THE
FATHER'S
TOPICAL BIBLE

NEW INTERNATIONAL
VERSION

Tulsa, Oklahoma

Presented By:
Wisdom International
P. O. Box 747
Dallas, Texas 75221
214/518-1833

Published by
Honor Books
P. O. Box 55388
Tulsa, Oklahoma 74155

2nd Printing
Over 30,000 in Print

The Father's Topical Bible

All Scripture references are from
The Holy Bible, New International Version.
Copyright © 1973, 1978, 1984
by the International Bible Society.
Used by permission of Zondervan Bible Publishers.

ISBN 1-56292-016-2

Presented
to

_____

by

_____

_____

Date

Contents

Your Wife

Your Work

Your Daily Schedule

Your Finances

Your Church

Your Personal Needs

The Salvation Experience

There Are Three Basic Reasons To Believe the Bible Is the Infallible and Pure Word of God

1. *No human would have written a standard this high.* Think of the best person you know. You must admit he would have left certain scriptures out had he written the Bible. So the Bible projects an inhuman standard and way of life. It has to be God because no man you know would have ever written a standard that high.

2. *There is an aura, a climate, a charisma, a presence the Bible generates which no other book in the world creates.* Lay an encyclopedia on your table at the restaurant, nobody will look at you twice. But when you lay your Bible on the table, they will stare at you, watch you chew your food, and even read your license plate when you get in your car! Why? The Bible creates the presence of God and forces a reaction in the hearts of men.

3. *The nature of man is changed when he reads the Bible.* Men change. *Peace* enters into their spirits. Joy wells up within their lives. Men like what they become when they read this book. Men accept Christ, because this Bible says Jesus Christ is the Son of God and that all have sinned and the wages of sin will bring death; and the only forgiveness that they can find is through Jesus, the Son of God.

Three Basic Reasons for Accepting Christ

1. *You needed forgiveness.* At some point in your life, you will want to be clean. You will hate guilt; you will crave purity. You have a built-in desire toward God, and you will have to address that appetite at some point in your life.

2. *You need a friend.* You may be sitting there saying, "But, don't I have friends?" Yes, but you have never had a friend like Jesus. Nobody can handle the information about your life as well as He can. He is the most consistent relationship you will ever know. Human friends vacillate in their reaction, depending on your mood or theirs.

Jesus Christ never changes his opinion of you. Nobody can tell Him anything which will change His mind about you. You cannot enjoy His world without His companionship.

3. *You needed a future.* All men have a built-in need for immortality, a craving for an eternity. God placed it within us. D.L. Moody once made a statement, "One of these days you are going to hear that I'm dead and gone. When you do, don't believe a word of it. I'll be more alive then, than at any other time in my life." Each of us wonders about eternity. What is death like? What happens when I die? Is there a hell? a heaven? a God? a devil? What happens? Every man wants to be around tomorrow. The only guarantee you will have of a future is to have the Eternal One on the inside of you. *He is Jesus Christ, the Son of God!*

The Gospel means Good News, you can change; your sins can be forgiven; your guilt can be dissolved; God loves *you*! He wants to be the difference in your life. All have sinned and come short of the glory of God." Romans 3:23. "The wages of sin is death." Romans 6:23. You might say, what does that mean?

It means that all unconfessed sin will be judged and penalized, but that is not the end of the story. The second part of verse 23 says "but the gift of God is eternal life through Jesus Christ our Lord." What does that mean? It means that between the wrath and judgment of God upon your sin, Jesus Christ the Son of God stepped in and absorbed your judgment and your penalty for you. God says if you recognize and respect Him and His worth as the Son of God, judgment will be withheld, and you will receive a pardon, forgiveness of all your mistakes.

What do you have to do? "If you believe in your heart that Jesus is the Son of God and that God raised him from the dead on the third day, and confess that with your mouth, then you will be saved." Romans 10:9-10. What does the word "saved" mean? *Removed from danger.* It simply means if you respect and recognize the worth of Jesus Christ, God will take you out of the danger zone and receive you as a child of the Most High God. What is His gift that you are to receive? His Son. "For God so loved the world that he gave his only begotten Son, that whosoever believeth in Him should not perish but have everlasting

Life.'' John 3:16. How do you accept His Son? Accept His mercy. How do you reject your sins? Confess them and turn away from them. ''If I confess my sins he is faithful and just to forgive me my sins and to cleanse me from all unrighteousness.'' 1 John 1:9. That is the Gospel.

Your Relationship
With God

Your Prayer Life

Look to the LORD and his strength; seek his face always.

1 Chronicles 16:11

If my people, who are called by my name, will humble themselves and pray and seek my face and turn from their wicked ways, then will I hear from heaven and will forgive their sin and will heal their land.

2 Chronicles 7:14

My heart says of you, "Seek his face!" Your face, LORD, I will seek.

Psalm 27:8

By day the LORD directs his love, at night his song is with me — a prayer to the God of my life.

Psalm 42:8

Look to the LORD and his strength; seek his face always.

Psalm 105:4

Seek the LORD while he may be found; call on him while he is near.

Isaiah 55:6

But when you pray, go into your room, close the door and pray to your Father, who is unseen. Then your Father, who sees what is done in secret, will reward you.

And when you pray, do not keep on babbling like pagans, for they think they will be heard because of their many words.

Do not be like them, for your Father knows what you need before you ask him.

This, then, is how you should pray: "Our Father in heaven, hallowed be your name."

Matthew 6:6-9

If you believe, you will receive whatever you ask for in prayer.

Matthew 21:22

Watch and pray so that you will not fall into temptation. The spirit is willing, but the body is weak.

Matthew 26:41

Very early in the morning, while it was still dark, Jesus got up, left the house and went off to a solitary place, where he prayed.

Mark 1:35

Therefore I tell you, whatever you ask for in prayer, believe that you have received it, and it will be yours.

Mark 11:24

Be on guard! Be alert! You do not know when that time will come.

Mark 13:33

Then Jesus told his disciples a parable to show them that they should always pray and not give up.

Luke 18:1

Be always on the watch, and pray that you may be able to escape all that is about to happen, and that you may be able to stand before the Son of Man.

Luke 21:36

In the same way, the Spirit helps us in our weakness. We do not know what we ought to pray for, but the Spirit himself intercedes for us with groans that words cannot express.

Romans 8:26

Be joyful in hope, patient in affliction, faithful in prayer.

Romans 12:12

And pray in the Spirit on all occasions with all kinds of prayers and requests. With this in mind, be alert and always keep on praying for all the saints.

Ephesians 6:18

Do not be anxious about anything, but in everything, by prayer and petition, with thanksgiving, present your requests to God.

Philippians 4:6

Devote yourselves to prayer, being watchful and thankful.

Colossians 4:2

Pray continually.

1 Thessalonians 5:17

I want men everywhere to lift up holy hands in prayer, without anger or disputing.
1 Timothy 2:8

Let us then approach the throne of grace with confidence, so that we may receive mercy and find grace to help us in our time of need.
Hebrews 4:16

For the eyes of the Lord are on the righteous and his ears are attentive to their prayer, but the face of the Lord is against those who do evil.
1 Peter 3:12

But you, dear friends, build yourselves up in your most holy faith and pray in the Holy Spirit.
Jude 1:20

Your Study of God's Word

Do not add to what I command you and do not subtract from it, but keep the commands of the LORD your God that I give you.
Deuteronomy 4:2

These commandments that I give you today are to be upon your hearts.

Deuteronomy 6:6

The secret things belong to the LORD our God, but the things revealed belong to us and to our children forever, that we may follow all the words of this law.

Deuteronomy 29:29

No, the word is very near you; it is in your mouth and in your heart so you may obey it.

Deuteronomy 30:14

Do not let this Book of the Law depart from your mouth; meditate on it day and night, so that you may be careful to do everything written in it. Then you will be prosperous and successful.

Joshua 1:8

He remembers his covenant forever, the word he commanded, for a thousand generations.

1 Chronicles 16:15

Accept instruction from his mouth and lay up his words in your heart.

Job 22:22

I have not departed from the commands of his lips; I have treasured the words of his mouth more than my daily bread.

Job 23:12

Blessed is the man who does not walk in the counsel of the wicked or stand in the way of sinners or sit in the seat of mockers.
But his delight is in the law of the LORD, and on his law he meditates day and night.

Psalm 1:1,2

The law of the LORD is perfect, reviving the soul. The statutes of the LORD are trustworthy, making wise the simple.

Psalm 19:7

I will instruct you and teach you in the way you should go; I will counsel you and watch over you.

Psalm 32:8

The law of his God is in his heart; his feet do not slip.

Psalm 37:31

How can a young man keep his way pure? By living according to your word.

I have hidden your word in my heart that I might not sin against you.

Your word is a lamp to my feet and a light for my path.

Psalm 119:9,11,105

When you walk, they will guide you; when you sleep, they will watch over you; when you awake, they will speak to you.

For these commands are a lamp, this teaching is a light, and the corrections of discipline are the way to life.

Proverbs 6:22,23

Commit to the LORD whatever you do, and your plans will succeed.

Proverbs 16:3

Whether you turn to the right or to the left, your ears will hear a voice behind you, saying, "This is the way; walk in it."

Isaiah 30:21

The grass withers and the flowers fall, but the word of our God stands forever.

Isaiah 40:8

Therefore everyone who hears these words of mine and puts them into practice is like a wise man who built his house on the rock.

Matthew 7:24

Jesus replied, "You are in error because you do not know the Scriptures or the power of God."

Matthew 22:29

Heaven and earth will pass away, but my words will never pass away.

Mark 13:31

To the Jews who had believed him, Jesus said, "If you hold to my teaching, you are really my disciples.

Then you will know the truth, and the truth will set you free."

John 8:31,32

Consequently, faith comes from hearing the message, and the message is heard through the word of Christ.

Romans 10:17

All Scripture is God-breathed and is useful for teaching, rebuking, correcting and training in righteousness, so that the man of God may be thoroughly equipped for every good work.

2 Timothy 3:16,17

Through these he has given us his very great and precious promises, so that through them you may participate in the divine nature and escape the corruption in the world caused by evil desires.

For prophecy never had its origin in the will of man, but men spoke from God as they were carried along by the Holy Spirit.

2 Peter 1:4,21

Your Attitude Toward Praise and Worship

With praise and thanksgiving they sang to the LORD: "He is good; his love to Israel endures forever." And all the people gave a great shout of praise to the LORD, because the foundation of the house of the LORD was laid.

Ezra 3:11

But I, by your great mercy, will come into your house; in reverence will I bow down toward your holy temple.

Psalm 5:7

I will give you thanks in the great assembly; among throngs of people I will praise you.

Psalm 35:18

Blessed are those who dwell in your house; they are ever praising you. Selah.

Psalm 84:4

It is good to praise the LORD and make music to your name, O Most High, to proclaim your love in the morning and your faithfulness at night.

Psalm 92:1,2

Come, let us bow down in worship, let us kneel before the LORD our Maker.

Psalm 95:6

Shout for joy to the LORD, all the earth.

Worship the LORD with gladness; come before him with joyful songs.

Know that the LORD is God. It is he who made us, and we are his; we are his people, the sheep of his pasture.

Enter his gates with thanksgiving and his courts with praise; give thanks to him and praise his name.

Psalm 100:1-4

Let them give thanks to the LORD for his unfailing love and his wonderful deeds for men.

Let them exalt him in the assembly of the people and praise him in the council of the elders.

Psalm 107:8,32

I will bow down toward your holy temple and will praise your name for your love and your faithfulness, for you have exalted above all things your name and your word.

Psalm 138:2

Praise the LORD. Praise God in his sanctuary; praise him in his mighty heavens.

Praise him for his acts of power; praise him for his surpassing greatness.

Praise him with the sounding of the trumpet, praise him with the harp and lyre; praise him with the clash of cymbals, praise him with resounding cymbals.

Let everything that has breath praise the LORD. Praise the LORD.

Psalm 150:1-3,5,6

Surely God is my salvation; I will trust and not be afraid. The LORD, the LORD, is my strength and my song; he has become my salvation.

Isaiah 12:2

Sing for joy, O heavens, for the LORD has done this; shout aloud, O earth beneath. Burst into song, you mountains, you forests and all your trees, for the LORD has redeemed Jacob, he displays his glory in Israel.

Isaiah 44:23

Jesus said to him, ''Away from me, Satan! For it is written: 'Worship the Lord your God, and serve him only.'''

Matthew 4:10

Jesus answered, ''It is written: 'Worship the Lord your God and serve him only.' ''

Luke 4:8

Yet a time is coming and has now come when the true worshipers will worship the Father in spirit and truth, for they are the kind of worshipers the Father seeks.

God is spirit, and his worshipers must worship in spirit and in truth.

John 4:23,24

We know that God does not listen to sinners. He listens to the godly man who does his will.

John 9:31

So what shall I do? I will pray with my spirit, but I will also pray with my mind; I will sing with my spirit, but I will also sing with my mind.

1 Corinthians 14:15

For it is we who are the circumcision, we who worship by the Spirit of God, who glory in Christ Jesus, and who put no confidence in the flesh.

Philippians 3:3

Devote yourselves to prayer, being watchful and thankful.

Colossians 4:2

I want men everywhere to lift up holy hands in prayer, without anger or disputing.

1 Timothy 2:8

Your Hourly Obedience

So if you faithfully obey the commands I am giving you today — to love the LORD your God and to serve him with all your heart and with all your soul — then I will send rain on your land in its season, both autumn and spring rains, so that you may gather in your grain, new wine and oil.

Deuteronomy 11:13,14

If you listen carefully to what he says and do all that I say, I will be an enemy to your enemies and will oppose those who oppose you.

My angel will go ahead of you.

Exodus 23:22,23a

And if you walk in my ways and obey my statutes and commands as David your father did, I will give you a long life.

1 Kings 3:14

Blessed is the man who does not walk in the counsel of the wicked or stand in the way of sinners or sit in the seat of mockers.

But his delight is in the law of the LORD, and on his law he meditates day and night.

Psalm 1:1,2

All the ways of the LORD are loving and faithful for those who keep the demands of his covenant.

Psalm 25:10

The fear of the LORD is the beginning of wisdom; all who follow his precepts have good understanding. To him belongs eternal praise.
Psalm 111:10

Blessed are they who keep his statutes and seek him with all their heart.

You have laid down precepts that are to be fully obeyed.
Psalm 119:2,4

Keep my commands and you will live; guard my teachings as the apple of your eye.
Proverbs 7:2

He who obeys instructions guards his life, but he who is contemptuous of his ways will die.
Proverbs 19:16

If you are willing and obedient, you will eat the best from the land.
Isaiah 1:19

Anyone who breaks one of the least of these commandments and teaches others to do the same will be called least in the kingdom of heaven, but whoever practices and teaches these commands will be called great in the kingdom of heaven.

Matthew 5:19

For whoever does the will of my Father in heaven is my brother and sister and mother.
Matthew 12:50

Whoever can be trusted with very little can also be trusted with much, and whoever is dishonest with very little will also be dishonest with much.

So if you have not been trustworthy in handling worldly wealth, who will trust you with true riches?

And if you have not been trustworthy with someone else's property, who will give you property of your own?

Luke 16:10-12

"If you love me, you will obey what I command."

Jesus replied, "If anyone loves me, he will obey my teaching. My Father will love him, and we will come to him and make our home with him."

John 14:15,23

If you obey my commands, you will remain in my love, just as I have obeyed my Father's commands and remain in his love.

You are my friends if you do what I command.

John 15:10,14

Peter and the other apostles replied: "We must obey God rather than men!"

Acts 5:29

Although he was a son, he learned obedience from what he suffered and, once made perfect, he became the source of eternal salvation for all who obey him.

Hebrews 5:8,9

Submit yourselves, then, to God. Resist the devil, and he will flee from you.

James 4:7

And receive from him anything we ask, because we obey his commands and do what pleases him.

Those who obey his commands live in him, and he in them. And this is how we know that he lives in us: We know it by the Spirit he gave us.

1 John 3:22,24

Your Attitude

The Loving Father

Hatred stirs up dissension, but love covers over all wrongs.

Proverbs 10:12

Give to the one who asks you, and do not turn away from the one who wants to borrow from you.

Matthew 5:42

A new command I give you: Love one another. As I have loved you, so you must love one another.

By this all men will know that you are my disciples, if you love one another.

John 13:34,35

As the Father has loved me, so have I loved you. Now remain in my love.

If you obey my commands, you will remain in my love, just as I have obeyed my Father's commands and remain in his love.

My command is this: Love each other as I have loved you.

Greater love has no one than this, that he lay down his life for his friends.

You are my friends if you do what I command.

This is my command: Love each other.
John 15:9,10,12-14,17

Let no debt remain outstanding, except the continuing debt to love one another, for he who loves his fellowman has fulfilled the law.

Love does no harm to its neighbor. Therefore love is the fulfillment of the law.
Romans 13:8,10

If I speak in the tongues of men and of angels, but have not love, I am only a resounding gong or a clanging cymbal.

If I have the gift of prophecy and can fathom all mysteries and all knowledge, and if I have a faith that can move mountains, but have not love, I am nothing.

If I give all I possess to the poor and surrender my body to the flames, but have not love, I gain nothing.

Love is patient, love is kind. It does not envy, it does not boast, it is not proud.

It is not rude, it is not self-seeking, it is not easily angered, it keeps no record of wrongs.

It always protects, always trusts, always hopes, always perseveres.

Love never fails.

1 Corinthians 13:1-5,7,8a

And now these three remain: faith, hope and love. But the greatest of these is love.

1 Corinthians 13:13

This is the message you heard from the beginning: We should love one another.

We know that we have passed from death to life, because we love our brothers. Anyone who does not love remains in death.

Dear children, let us not love with words or tongue but with actions and in truth.
1 John 3:11,14,18

Dear friends, let us love one another, for love comes from God. Everyone who loves has been born of God and knows God.

Whoever does not love does not know God, because God is love.
1 John 4:7,8

The Understanding Father

I will praise the LORD, who counsels me; even at night my heart instructs me.
Psalm 16:7

As for God, his way is perfect; the word of the LORD is flawless. He is a shield for all who take refuge in him.
Psalm 18:30

Teach me your way, O LORD; lead me in a straight path because of my oppressors.

Psalm 27:11

Send forth your light and your truth, let them guide me; let them bring me to your holy mountain, to the place where you dwell.

Psalm 43:3

The LORD will fulfill for me; your love, O LORD, endures forever — do not abandon the works of your hands.

Psalm 138:8

Trust in the LORD with all your heart and lean not on your own understanding; in all your ways acknowledge him, and he will make your paths straight.

Proverbs 3:5,6

Counsel and sound judgment are mine; I have understanding and power.

Proverbs 8:14

Understanding is a fountain of life to those who have it, but folly brings punishment to fools.

A wise man's heart guides his mouth, and his lips promote instruction.

Proverbs 16:22,23

By wisdom a house is built, and through understanding it is established; through knowledge its rooms are filled with rare and beautiful treasures.

Proverbs 24:3,4

"For my thoughts are not your thoughts, neither are your ways my ways," declares the LORD.

"As the heavens are higher than the earth, so are my ways higher than your ways and my thoughts than your thoughts."

Isaiah 55:8,9

Call to me and I will answer you and tell you great and unsearchable things you do not know.

Jeremiah 33:3

Then he opened their minds so they could understand the Scriptures.

Luke 24:45

The Patient Father

But as for you, be strong and do not give up, for your work will be rewarded.

2 Chronicles 15:7

Wait for the LORD; be strong and take heart and wait for the LORD.

Psalm 27:14

Be still before the LORD and wait patiently for him; do not fret when men succeed in their ways, when they carry out their wicked schemes.

Psalm 37:7

I waited patiently for the LORD; he turned to me and heard my cry.

Psalm 40:1

For you have been my hope, O Sovereign LORD, my confidence since my youth.
Psalm 71:5

The end of a matter is better than its beginning, and patience is better than pride.

Do not be quickly provoked in your spirit, for anger resides in the lap of fools.
Ecclesiastes 7:8,9

But those who hope in the LORD will renew their strength. They will soar on wings like eagles; they will run and not grow weary, they will walk and not be faint.
Isaiah 40:31

But blessed is the man who trusts in the LORD, whose confidence is in him.
Jeremiah 17:7

By standing firm you will gain life.
Luke 21:19

Not only so, but we also rejoice in our sufferings, because we know that suffering produces perseverance; perseverance, character; and character, hope.

And hope does not disappoint us, because God has poured out his love into our hearts by the Holy Spirit, whom he has given us.

Romans 5:3-5

But if we hope for what we do not yet have, we wait for it patiently.

Romans 8:25

For everything that was written in the past was written to teach us, so that through endurance and the encouragement of the Scriptures we might have hope.

May the God who gives endurance and encouragement give you a spirit of unity among yourselves as you follow Christ Jesus.

May the God of hope fill you with all joy and peace as you trust in him, so that you may overflow with hope by the power of the Holy Spirit.

Romans 15:4,5,13

But the fruit of the Spirit is love, joy, peace, patience, kindness, goodness, faithfulness.

Galatians 5:22

I can do everything through him who gives me strength.

Philippians 4:13

We do not want you to become lazy, but to imitate those who through faith and patience inherit what has been promised.

Hebrews 6:12

So do not throw away your confidence; it will be richly rewarded.

You need to persevere so that when you have done the will of God, you will receive what he has promised.

For in just a very little while, He who is coming will come and will not delay.

Hebrews 10:35-37

Because you know that the testing of your faith develops perseverance.

Perseverance must finish its work so that you may be mature and complete, not lacking anything.

James 1:3,4

Be patient, then, brothers, until the Lord's coming. See how the farmer waits for the land to yield its valuable crop and how patient he is for the autumn and spring rains.

You too, be patient and stand firm, because the Lord's coming is near.

James 5:7,8

The Self-Controlled Father

Now go; I will help you speak and will teach you what to say.

Exodus 4:12

Teach me, and I will be quiet; show me where I have been wrong.

Job 6:24

Who can discern his errors? Forgive my hidden faults.

Psalm 19:12

''If you are willing and obedient, you will eat the best from the land; but if you resist and rebel, you will be devoured by the sword.'' For the mouth of the LORD has spoken.

Isaiah 1:19,20

Because the Sovereign LORD helps me, I will not be disgraced. Therefore have I set my face like flint, and I know I will not be put to shame.

Isaiah 50:7

"The glory of this present house will be greater than the glory of the former house," says the LORD Almighty. "And in this place I will grant peace," declares the LORD Almighty.

Haggai 2:9

For out of the overflow of the heart the mouth speaks.

But I tell you that men will have to give account on the day of judgment for every careless word they have spoken.

For by your words you will be acquitted, and by your words you will be condemned.

Matthew 12:34b,36,37

I tell you the truth, whatever you bind on earth will be bound in heaven, and whatever you loose on earth will be loosed in heaven.

Matthew 18:18

The expert in the law replied, ''The one who had mercy on him.'' Jesus told him, ''Go and do likewise.''

Luke 10:37

Slaves, obey your earthly masters with respect and fear, and with sincerity of heart, just as you would obey Christ.

Serve wholeheartedly, as if you were serving the Lord, not men.

Ephesians 6:5,7

Therefore, prepare your minds for action; be self-controlled; set your hope fully on the grace to be given you when Jesus Christ is revealed.

As obedient children, do not conform to the evil desires you had when you lived in ignorance.

1 Peter 1:13,14

Submit yourselves for the Lord's sake to every authority instituted among men: whether to the king, as the supreme authority, or to governors, who are sent by him to punish those who do wrong and to commend those who do right.

For it is God's will that by doing good you should silence the ignorant talk of foolish men.
1 Peter 2:13-15

You, dear children, are from God and have overcome them, because the one who is in you is greater than the one who is in the world.

We are from God, and whoever knows God listens to us; but whoever is not from God does not listen to us. This is how we recognize the Spirit of truth and the spirit of falsehood.

And so we know and rely on the love God has for us. God is love. Whoever lives in love lives in God, and God in him.

In this way, love is made complete among us so that we will have confidence on the day of judgment, because in this world we are like him.

1 John 4:4,6,16,17

The Listening Father

The heart of the discerning acquires knowledge; the ears of the wise seek it out.

Proverbs 18:15

Therefore hear the word of the LORD, you scoffers who rule this people in Jerusalem.

Isaiah 28:14

The man said to me, "Son of man, look with your eyes and hear with your ears and pay attention to everything I am going to show you."

Ezekiel 40:4a

But everyone who hears these words of mine and does not put them into practice is like a foolish man who built his house on sand.

The rain came down, the streams rose, and the winds blew and beat against that house, and it fell with a great crash.

Matthew 7:26,27

But blessed are your eyes because they see, and your ears because they hear.

Matthew 13:16

Therefore consider carefully how you listen. Whoever has will be given more; whoever does not have, even what he thinks he has will be taken from him.

Luke 8:18

He who belongs to God hears what God says. The reason you do not hear is that you do not belong to God.

John 8:47

"You are a king, then!" said Pilate. Jesus answered, "You are right in saying I am a king. In fact, for this reason I was born, and for this I came into the world, to testify to the truth. Everyone on the side of truth listens to me."

John 18:37

Do not merely listen to the word, and so deceive yourselves. Do what it says.

Anyone who listens to the word but does not do what it says is like a man who looks at his face in a mirror.

But the man who looks intently into the perfect law that gives freedom, and continues to do this, not forgetting what he has heard, but doing it — he will be blessed in what he does.

James 1:22,23,25

He who has an ear, let him hear what the Spirit says to the churches.

Revelation 2:29

The Teaching Father

Now go; I will help you speak and will teach you what to say.

Exodus 4:12

Teach me, and I will be quiet; show me where I have been wrong.

Job 6:24

Show me your ways, O LORD, teach me your paths; guide me in your truth and teach me, for you are God my Savior, and my hope is in you all day long.

He guides the humble in what is right and teaches them his way.

Who, then, is the man that fears the LORD? He will instruct him in the way chosen for him.

Psalm 25:4,5,9,12

Teach me your way, O LORD; lead me in a straight path because of my oppressors.

Psalm 27:11

I will instruct you and teach you in the way you should go; I will counsel you and watch over you.

Psalm 32:8

I recounted my ways and you answered me; teach me your decrees.

Let me understand the teaching of your precepts; then I will meditate on your wonders.

Psalm 119:26,27

Teach me to do your will, for you are my God; may your good Spirit lead me on level ground.

Psalm 143:10

He who walks with the wise grows wise, but a companion of fools suffers harm.

Proverbs 13:20

When a mocker is punished, the simple gain wisdom; when a wise man is instructed, he gets knowledge.

Proverbs 21:11

I know, O LORD, that a man's life is not his own; it is not for man to direct his steps.

Jeremiah 10:23

Call to me and I will answer you and tell you great and unsearchable things you do not know.

Jeremiah 33:3

He told them, ''The secret of the kingdom of God has been given to you. But to those on the outside everything is said in parables.''

Mark 4:11

I have set you an example that you should do as I have done for you.

John 13:15

Be imitators of God, therefore, as dearly loved children and live a life of love, just as Christ loved us and gave himself up for us as a fragrant offering and sacrifice to God.

Ephesians 5:1,2

Because you know that the Lord will reward everyone for whatever good he does, whether he is slave or free.

Ephesians 6:8

And we also thank God continually because, when you received the word of God, which you heard from us, you accepted it not as the word of men, but as it actually is, the word of God, which is at work in you who believe.

1 Thessalonians 2:13

In fact, though by this time you ought to be teachers, you need someone to teach you the elementary truths of God's word all over again. You need milk, not solid food!

Anyone who lives on milk, being still an infant, is not acquainted with the teaching about righteousness.

Hebrews 5:12,13

Whoever claims to live in him must walk as Jesus did.

1 John 2:6

The Approachable Father

The law of the LORD is perfect, reviving the soul. The statutes of the LORD are trustworthy, making wise the simple.

The precepts of the LORD are right, giving joy to the heart. The commands of the LORD are radiant, giving light to the eyes.

The fear of the LORD is pure, enduring forever. The ordinances of the LORD are sure and altogether righteous.

They are more precious than gold, than much pure gold; they are sweeter than honey, than honey from the comb.

May the words of my mouth and the meditation of my heart be pleasing in your sight, O LORD, my Rock and my Redeemer.

Psalm 19:7-10,14

Guide me in your truth and teach me, for you are God my Savior, and my hope is in you all day long.

He guides the humble in what is right and teaches them his way.

Psalm 25:5,9

Teach me your way, O LORD; lead me in a straight path.

Psalm 27:11a

Trust in him at all times, O people; pour out your hearts to him, for God is our refuge. Selah.

Psalm 62:8

You guide me with your counsel, and afterward you will take me into glory.

Psalm 73:24

Then you will call, and the LORD will answer; you will cry for help, and he will say: Here am I. If you do away with the yoke of oppression, with the pointing finger and malicious talk, and if you spend yourselves in behalf of the hungry and satisfy the needs of the oppressed, then your light will rise in the darkness, and your night will become like the noonday.

The LORD will guide you always; he will satisfy your needs in a sun-scorched land and will strengthen your frame. You will be like a well-watered garden, like a spring whose waters never fail.

Isaiah 58:9-11

The Spirit of the Sovereign LORD is on me, because the LORD has anointed me to preach good news to the poor. He has sent me to bind up the brokenhearted, to proclaim freedom for the captives and release from darkness for the prisoners.

And you will be called priests of the LORD, you will be named ministers of our God. You will feed on the wealth of nations, and in their riches you will boast.

Isaiah 61:1,6

You are the salt of the earth. But if the salt loses its saltiness, how can it be made salty again? It is no longer good for anything, except to be thrown out and trampled by men.

You are the light of the world. A city on a hill cannot be hidden.

Neither do people light a lamp and put it under a bowl. Instead they put it on its stand, and it gives light to everyone in the house.

In the same way, let your light shine before men, that they may see your good deeds and praise your Father in heaven.

Matthew 5:13-16

For I was hungry and you gave me something to eat, I was thirsty and you gave me something to drink, I was a stranger and you invited me in, I needed clothes and you clothed me, I was sick and you looked after me, I was in prison and you came to visit me.

Then the righteous will answer him, "Lord, when did we see you hungry and feed you, or thirsty and give you something to drink?

When did we see you a stranger and invite you in, or needing clothes and clothe you?

When did we see you sick or in prison and go to visit you?"

The King will reply, "I tell you the truth, whatever you did for one of the least of these brothers of mine, you did for me."

Matthew 25:35-40

He said to them, "Go into all the world and preach the good news to all creation."

Mark 16:15

But you will receive power when the Holy Spirit comes on you; and you will be my witnesses in Jerusalem, and in all Judea and Samaria, and to the ends of the earth.

Acts 1:8

The Godly Father

He who walks with the wise grows wise, but a companion of fools suffers harm.

Proverbs 13:20

And if anyone gives even a cup of cold water to one of these little ones because he is my disciple, I tell you the truth, he will certainly not lose his reward.

Matthew 10:42

Just as the Son of Man did not come to be served, but to serve, and to give his life as a ransom for many.

Matthew 20:28

Not so with you. Instead, whoever wants to become great among you must be your servant, and whoever wants to be first must be slave of all.

Mark 10:43,44

The expert in the law replied, ''The one who had mercy on him.'' Jesus told him, ''Go and do likewise.''

Luke 10:37

I tell you the truth, no servant is greater than his master, nor is a messenger greater than the one who sent him.

A new command I give you: Love one another. As I have loved you, so you must love one another.

John 13:16,34

May the God who gives endurance and encouragement give you a spirit of unity among yourselves as you follow Christ Jesus, so that with one heart and mouth you may glorify the God and Father of our Lord Jesus Christ.

Accept one another, then, just as Christ accepted you, in order to bring praise to God.
Romans 15:5-7

Now it is required that those who have been given a trust must prove faithful.
1 Corinthians 4:2

Therefore, my dear brothers, stand firm. Let nothing move you. Always give yourselves fully to the work of the Lord, because you know that your labor in the Lord is not in vain.
1 Corinthians 15:58

Carry each other's burdens, and in this way you will fulfill the law of Christ.

Therefore, as we have opportunity, let us do good to all people, especially to those who belong to the family of believers.
Galatians 6:2,10

Be imitators of God, therefore, as dearly loved children and live a life of love, just as

Christ loved us and gave himself up for us as a fragrant offering and sacrifice to God.

Ephesians 5:1,2

Slaves, obey your earthly masters with respect and fear, and with sincerity of heart, just as you would obey Christ.

Serve wholeheartedly, as if you were serving the Lord, not men.

Ephesians 6:5,7

Your attitude should be the same as that of Christ Jesus:

Who, being in very nature God, did not consider equality with God something to be grasped, but made himself nothing, taking the very nature of a servant, being made in human likeness.

And being found in appearance as a man, he humbled himself and became obedient to death — even death on a cross!

Philippians 2:5-8

Bear with each other and forgive whatever grievances you may have against one another. Forgive as the Lord forgave you.

Slaves, obey your earthly masters in everything; and do it, not only when their eye is on you and to win their favor, but with sincerity of heart and reverence for the Lord.
Colossians 3:13,22

Let us fix our eyes on Jesus, the author and perfecter of our faith, who for the joy set before him endured the cross, scorning its shame, and sat down at the right hand of the throne of God.

Consider him who endured such opposition from sinful men, so that you will not grow weary and lose heart.
Hebrews 12:2,3

To this you were called, because Christ suffered for you, leaving you an example, that you should follow in his steps.
1 Peter 2:21

The Father of Integrity

Let God weigh me in honest scales and he will know that I am blameless.

Job 31:6

Blessed is the man who does not walk in the counsel of the wicked or stand in the way of sinners or sit in the seat of mockers.

But his delight is in the law of the LORD, and on his law he meditates day and night.

Psalm 1:1,2

All the ways of the LORD are loving and faithful for those who keep the demands of his covenant.

Psalm 25:10

Vindicate me, O LORD, for I have led a blameless life; I have trusted in the LORD without wavering.

Psalm 26:1

In my integrity you uphold me and set me in your presence forever.

Psalm 41:12

And David shepherded them with integrity of heart; with skillful hands he led them.

Psalm 78:72

The fear of the LORD is the beginning of wisdom; all who follow his precepts have good understanding. To him belongs eternal praise.

Psalm 111:10

Blessed are they who keep his statutes and seek him with all their heart.

You have laid down precepts that are to be fully obeyed.

Psalm 119:2,4

The integrity of the upright guides them, but the unfaithful are destroyed by their duplicity.

Proverbs 11:3

Better a poor man whose walk is blameless than a fool whose lips are perverse.

He who obeys instructions guards his life, but he who is contemptuous of his ways will die.

Proverbs 19:1,16

The righteous man leads a blameless life; blessed are his children after him.

Proverbs 20:7

If you are willing and obedient, you will eat the best from the land.

Isaiah 1:19

Do not repay anyone evil for evil. Be careful to do what is right in the eyes of everybody.

Romans 12:17

Finally, brothers, whatever is true, whatever is noble, whatever is right, whatever is pure, whatever is lovely, whatever is admirable — if anything is excellent or praiseworthy — think about such things.

Philippians 4:8

The Father Who Is a Leader

As for you, if you walk before me in integrity of heart and uprightness, as David your father did, and do all I command and observe my decrees and laws, I will establish your royal throne over Israel forever, as I promised David your father when I said, "You shall never fail to have a man on the throne of Israel."

1 Kings 9:4,5

If the LORD delights in a man's way, he makes his steps firm.

Psalm 37:23

For the LORD God is a sun and shield; the LORD bestows favor and honor; no good thing does he withhold from those whose walk is blameless.

Psalm 84:11

Good will come to him who is generous and lends freely, who conducts his affairs with justice.

Psalm 112:5

Better a little with righteousness than much gain with injustice.

In his heart a man plans his course, but the LORD determines his steps.

Proverbs 16:8,9

The LORD abhors dishonest scales, but accurate weights are his delight.

Proverbs 11:1

Whether you turn to the right or to the left, your ears will hear a voice behind you, saying, "This is the way; walk in it."

Isaiah 30:21

This is what the LORD Almighty says: "Administer true justice; show mercy and compassion to one another.

Do not oppress the widow or the fatherless, the alien or the poor. In your hearts do not think evil of each other."

Zechariah 7:9,10

For in the same way you judge others, you will be judged, and with the measure you use, it will be measured to you.

Matthew 7:2

But when he, the Spirit of truth, comes, he will guide you into all truth. He will not speak on his own; he will speak only what he hears, and he will tell you what is yet to come.

John 16:13

Peter and the other apostles replied: "We must obey God rather than men!"

Acts 5:29

Because those who are led by the Spirit of God are sons of God.

Romans 8:14

For kings and all those in authority, that we may live peaceful and quiet lives in all godliness and holiness.

1 Timothy 2:2

Submit yourselves for the Lord's sake to every authority instituted among men: whether to the king, as the supreme authority, or to governors, who are sent by him to punish those who do wrong and to commend those who do right.

For it is God's will that by doing good you should silence the ignorant talk of foolish men.

1 Peter 2:13-15

The Disciplinarian Father

Show me your ways, O LORD, teach me your paths.

Who, then, is the man that fears the LORD? He will instruct him in the way chosen for him.

Psalm 25:4,12

Teach me your way, O LORD; lead me in a straight path because of my oppressors.

I am still confident of this: I will see the goodness of the LORD in the land of the living.

Wait for the LORD; be strong and take heart and wait for the LORD.

Psalm 27:11,13,14

The LORD is my strength and my shield; my heart trusts in him, and I am helped. My heart leaps for joy and I will give thanks to him in song.

Psalm 28:7

Cast your cares on the LORD and he will sustain you; he will never let the righteous fall.

Psalm 55:22

Though I walk in the midst of trouble, you preserve my life; you stretch out your hand against the anger of my foes, with your right hand you save me.

Psalm 138:7

Teach me to do your will, for you are my God; may your good Spirit lead me on level ground.

Psalm 143:10

Keep my commands and you will live; guard my teachings as the apple of your eye.

Proverbs 7:2

Do not answer a fool according to his folly, or you will be like him yourself.

Proverbs 26:4

"If you are willing and obedient, you will eat the best from the land; but if you resist and rebel, you will be devoured by the sword." For the mouth of the LORD has spoken.

Isaiah 1:19,20

Correct me, LORD, but only with justice — not in your anger, lest you reduce me to nothing.

Jeremiah 10:24

The expert in the law replied, "The one who had mercy on him." Jesus told him, "Go and do likewise."

Luke 10:37

Peter and the other apostles replied: "We must obey God rather than men!"

Acts 5:29

Slaves, obey your earthly masters with respect and fear, and with sincerity of heart, just as you would obey Christ.

Serve wholeheartedly, as· if you were serving the Lord, not men.

Ephesians 6:5,7

Therefore, prepare your minds for action; be self-controlled; set your hope fully on the grace to be given you when Jesus Christ is revealed.

As obedient children, do not conform to the evil desires you had when you lived in ignorance.

1 Peter 1:13,14

The Motivating Father

The LORD will grant that the enemies who rise up against you will be defeated before you. They will come at you from one direction but flee from you in seven.

Deuteronomy 28:7

Be strong and courageous. Do not be afraid or terrified because of them, for the LORD your God goes with you; he will never leave you nor forsake you.

Deuteronomy 31:6

As for me, far be it from me that I should sin against the LORD by failing to pray for you. And I will teach you the way that is good and right.

1 Samuel 12:23

"Don't be afraid," the prophet answered. "Those who are with us are more than those who are with them."

2 Kings 6:16

Through you we push back our enemies; through your name we trample our foes.

Psalm 44:5

It is better to heed a wise man's rebuke than to listen to the song of fools.

Ecclesiastes 7:5

For I am the LORD, your God, who takes hold of your right hand and says to you, Do not fear; I will help you.

Isaiah 41:13

The Spirit of the Sovereign LORD is on me, because the LORD has anointed me to preach good news to the poor. He has sent me to bind up the brokenhearted, to proclaim freedom for the captives and release from darkness for the prisoners.

Isaiah 61:1

Those who are wise will shine like the brightness of the heavens, and those who lead many to righteousness, like the stars for ever and ever.

Daniel 12:3

Ask and it will be given to you; seek and you will find; knock and the door will be opened to you.

For everyone who asks receives; he who seeks finds; and to him who knocks, the door will be opened.

Matthew 7:7,8

Then you will know the truth, and the truth will set you free.

So if the Son sets you free, you will be free indeed.

John 8:32,36

I tell you the truth, anyone who has faith in me will do what I have been doing. He will do even greater things than these, because I am going to the Father.

John 14:12

But you will receive power when the Holy Spirit comes on you; and you will be my witnesses in Jerusalem, and in all Judea and Samaria, and to the ends of the earth.

Acts 1:8

For it is light that makes everything visible. This is why it is said: "Wake up, O sleeper, rise from the dead, and Christ will shine on you."

Ephesians 5:14

I can do everything through him who gives me strength.

Philippians 4:13

Being strengthened with all power according to his glorious might so that you may have great endurance and patience, and joyfully giving thanks to the Father, who has qualified you to share in the inheritance of the saints in the kingdom of light.

Colossians 1:11,12

Be wise in the way you act toward outsiders; make the most of every opportunity.

Colossians 4:5

For this reason I remind you to fan into flame the gift of God, which is in you through the laying on of my hands.

2 Timothy 1:6

You, dear children, are from God and have overcome them, because the one who is in you is greater than the one who is in the world.

We are from God, and whoever knows God listens to us; but whoever is not from God does not listen to us. This is how we recognize the Spirit of truth and the spirit of falsehood.

And so we know and rely on the love God has for us. God is love. Whoever lives in love lives in God, and God in him.

In this way, love is made complete among us so that we will have confidence on the day of judgment, because in this world we are like him.

1 John 4:4,6,16,17

The Providing Father

Since you are my rock and my fortress, for the sake of your name lead and guide me.

Psalm 31:3

Trust in the LORD and do good; dwell in the land and enjoy safe pasture.

Delight yourself in the LORD and he will give you the desires of your heart.

Commit your way to the LORD; trust in him and he will do this:

He will make your righteousness shine like the dawn, the justice of your cause like the noonday sun.

For evil men will be cut off, but those who hope in the LORD will inherit the land.

I was young and now I am old, yet I have never seen the righteous forsaken or their children begging bread.

For the LORD loves the just and will not forsake his faithful ones. They will be protected forever, but the offspring of the wicked will be cut off.

Psalm 37:3-6,9,25,28

You have been a refuge for the poor, a refuge for the needy in his distress, a shelter from the storm and a shade from the heat. For the breath of the ruthless is like a storm driving against a wall.

Isaiah 25:4

I can do everything through him who gives me strength.

And my God will meet all your needs according to his glorious riches in Christ Jesus.
Philippians 4:13,19

If any of you lacks wisdom, he should ask God, who gives generously to all without finding fault, and it will be given to him.
James 1:5

But the wisdom that comes from heaven is first of all pure; then peace-loving, considerate, submissive, full of mercy and good fruit, impartial and sincere.

Peacemakers who sow in peace raise a harvest of righteousness.
James 3:17,18

The prayer of a righteous man is powerful and effective.

James 5:16b

The Faithful Father

And though she spoke to Joseph day after day, he refused to go to bed with her or even be with her.

One day he went into the house to attend to his duties, and none of the household servants was inside.

She caught him by his cloak and said, "Come to bed with me!" But he left his cloak in her hand and ran out of the house.

Genesis 39:10-12

My times are in your hands; deliver me from my enemies and from those who pursue me.

Let your face shine on your servant; save me in your unfailing love.

Psalm 31:15,16

You are my hiding place; you will protect me from trouble and surround me with songs of deliverance. Selah.

Psalm 32:7

For the LORD will be your confidence.
Proverbs 3:26a

But those who hope in the LORD will renew their strength. They will soar on wings like eagles; they will run and not grow weary, they will walk and not be faint.
Isaiah 40:31

So in everything, do to others what you would have them do to you, for this sums up the Law and the Prophets.
Matthew 7:12

Flee from sexual immorality. All other sins a man commits are outside his body, but he who sins sexually sins against his own body.
1 Corinthians 6:18

Be kind and compassionate to one another, forgiving each other, just as in Christ God forgave you.
Ephesians 4:32

Husbands, love your wives, just as Christ loved the church and gave himself up for her to make her holy, cleansing her by the washing with water through the word, and to present her to himself as a radiant church, without stain or wrinkle or any other blemish, but holy and blameless.

In this same way, husbands ought to love their wives as their own bodies. He who loves his wife loves himself.

After all, no one ever hated his own body, but he feeds and cares for it, just as Christ does the church — for we are members of his body.

''For this reason a man will leave his father and mother and be united to his wife, and the two will become one flesh.''

This is a profound mystery — but I am talking about Christ and the church.

However, each one of you also must love his wife as he loves himself, and the wife must respect her husband.

Ephesians 5:25-33

And the peace of God, which transcends all understanding, will guard your hearts and your minds in Christ Jesus.

Finally, brothers, whatever is true, whatever is noble, whatever is right, whatever is pure, whatever is lovely, whatever is admirable — if anything is excellent or praiseworthy — think about such things.

Philippians 4:7,8

Do not repay evil with evil or insult with insult, but with blessing, because to this you were called so that you may inherit a blessing.

1 Peter 3:9

The Considerate Father

Refrain from anger and turn from wrath; do not fret — it leads only to evil.

Psalm 37:8

Good will come to him who is generous and lends freely, who conducts his affairs with justice.

Psalm 112:5

A friend loves at all times, and a brother is born for adversity.

Proverbs 17:17

He who is kind to the poor lends to the LORD, and he will reward him for what he has done.

Proverbs 19:17

A generous man will himself be blessed, for he shares his food with the poor.

Proverbs 22:9

He who gives to the poor will lack nothing, but he who closes his eyes to them receives many curses.

Proverbs 28:27

So in everything, do to others what you would have them do to you, for this sums up the Law and the Prophets.

Matthew 7:12

Give, and it will be given to you. A good measure, pressed down, shaken together and running over, will be poured into your lap. For with the measure you use, it will be measured to you.

Luke 6:38

On the first day of every week, each one of you should set aside a sum of money in keeping with his income, saving it up, so that when I come no collections will have to be made.

1 Corinthians 16:2

Remember this: Whoever sows sparingly will also reap sparingly, and whoever sows generously will also reap generously.

Each man should give what he has decided in his heart to give, not reluctantly or under compulsion, for God loves a cheerful giver.

And God is able to make all grace abound to you, so that in all things at all times, having all that you need, you will abound in every good work.

2 Corinthians 9:6-8

Command those who are rich in this present world not to be arrogant nor to put their hope in wealth, which is so uncertain, but to put their hope in God, who richly provides us with everything for our enjoyment.

Command them to do good, to be rich in good deeds, and to be generous and willing to share.

In this way they will lay up treasure for themselves as a firm foundation for the coming age, so that they may take hold of the life that is truly life.

1 Timothy 6:17-19

If anyone has material possessions and sees his brother in need but has no pity on him, how can the love of God be in him?

Dear children, let us not love with words or tongue but with actions and in truth.

1 John 3:17,18

The Kind Father

Refrain from anger and turn from wrath; do not fret — it leads only to evil.

Psalm 37:8

A gentle answer turns away wrath, but a harsh word stirs up anger.

A hot-tempered man stirs up dissension, but a patient man calms a quarrel.

Proverbs 15:1,18

What a man desires is unfailing love; better to be poor than a liar.

Proverbs 19:22

Whoever has my commands and obeys them, he is the one who loves me. He who loves me will be loved by my Father, and I too will love him and show myself to him.

John 14:21

As the Father has loved me, so have I loved you. Now remain in my love.

If you obey my commands, you will remain in my love, just as I have obeyed my Father's commands and remain in his love.

My command is this: Love each other as I have loved you.

John 15:9,10,12

Rather, as servants of God we commend ourselves in every way: in great endurance; in troubles, hardships and distresses; in purity, understanding, patience and kindness; in the Holy Spirit and in sincere love.

2 Corinthians 6:4,6

Let us not become weary in doing good, for at the proper time we will reap a harvest if we do not give up.

Galatians 6:9

Get rid of all bitterness, rage and anger, brawling and slander, along with every form of malice.

Be kind and compassionate to one another, forgiving each other, just as in Christ God forgave you.

Ephesians 4:31,32

And we pray this in order that you may live a life worthy of the Lord and may please him in every way: bearing fruit in every good work, growing in the knowledge of God.

Colossians 1:10

Therefore, as God's chosen people, holy and dearly loved, clothe yourselves with compassion, kindness, humility, gentleness and patience.

Bear with each other and forgive whatever grievances you may have against one another. Forgive as the Lord forgave you.

Colossians 3:12,13

For this very reason, make every effort to add to your faith goodness; and to goodness, knowledge; and to knowledge, self-control; and to self-control, perseverance; and to perseverance, godliness; and to godliness, brotherly kindness; and to brotherly kindness, love.

For if you possess these qualities in increasing measure, they will keep you from being ineffective and unproductive in your knowledge of our Lord Jesus Christ.

2 Peter 1:5-8

Dear friends, let us love one another, for love comes from God. Everyone who loves has been born of God and knows God.

Whoever does not love does not know God, because God is love.

1 John 4:7,8

Your Child

When Your Child Becomes Rebellious Toward You

Now go; I will help you speak and will teach you what to say.

Exodus 4:12

To obey is better than sacrifice, and to heed is better than the fat of rams.

For rebellion is like the sin of divination, and arrogance like the evil of idolatry. Because you have rejected the word of the LORD, he has rejected you as king.

1 Samuel 15:22b,23

Teach me, and I will be quiet; show me where I have been wrong.

Job 6:24

Show me your ways, O LORD, teach me your paths.

Who, then, is the man that fears the LORD? He will instruct him in the way chosen for him.

Psalm 25:4,12

I am still confident of this: I will see the goodness of the LORD in the land of the living.
Wait for the LORD; be strong and take heart and wait for the LORD.

Psalm 27:13,14

The LORD is my strength and my shield; my heart trusts in him, and I am helped. My heart leaps for joy and I will give thanks to him in song.

Psalm 28:7

Cast your cares on the LORD and he will sustain you; he will never let the righteous fall.

Psalm 55:22

Though I walk in the midst of trouble, you preserve my life; you stretch out your hand against the anger of my foes, with your right hand you save me.

Psalm 138:7

Teach me to do your will, for you are my God; may your good Spirit lead me on level ground.

Psalm 143:10

Keep my commands and you will live; guard my teachings as the apple of your eye.

Proverbs 7:2

Do not answer a fool according to his folly, or you will be like him yourself.

Proverbs 26:4

If you are willing and obedient, you will eat the best from the land; but if you resist and rebel, you will be devoured by the sword. For the mouth of the LORD has spoken.

Isaiah 1:19,20

Can a mother forget the baby at her breast and have no compassion on the child she has borne? Though she may forget, I will not forget you!

Isaiah 49:15

I will give you the keys of the kingdom of heaven; whatever you bind on earth will be bound in heaven, and whatever you loose on earth will be loosed in heaven.

Matthew 16:19

Calling the Twelve to him, he sent them out two by two and gave them authority over evil spirits.

Mark 6:7

I have given you authority to trample on snakes and scorpions and to overcome all the power of the enemy; nothing will harm you.

Luke 10:19

So watch yourselves. If your brother sins, rebuke him, and if he repents, forgive him.

Luke 17:3

Peter and the other apostles replied: ''We must obey God rather than men!''

Acts 5:29

Fathers, do not exasperate your children; instead, bring them up in the training and instruction of the Lord.

Slaves, obey your earthly masters with respect and fear, and with sincerity of heart, just as you would obey Christ.

Serve wholeheartedly, as if you were serving the Lord, not men.

Ephesians 6:4,5,7

Therefore, prepare your minds for action; be self-controlled; set your hope fully on the grace to be given you when Jesus Christ is revealed.

As obedient children, do not conform to the evil desires you had when you lived in ignorance.

1 Peter 1:13,14

Submit yourselves for the Lord's sake to every authority instituted among men: whether to the king, as the supreme authority, or to governors, who are sent by him to punish those who do wrong and to commend those who do right.

For it is God's will that by doing good you should silence the ignorant talk of foolish men.

1 Peter 2:13-15

When Your Child Becomes Rebellious Toward God

Wait for the LORD; be strong and take heart and wait for the LORD.

Psalm 27:14

We wait in hope for the LORD; he is our help and our shield.

Psalm 33:20

Delight yourself in the LORD and he will give you the desires of your heart.
Commit your way to the LORD; trust in him and he will do this.

Psalm 37:4,5

Cast your cares on the LORD and he will sustain you; he will never let the righteous fall.

Psalm 55:22

For the LORD will not reject his people; he will never forsake his inheritance.

Psalm 94:14

I wait for the LORD, my soul waits, and in his word I put my hope.

Psalm 130:5

The LORD will fulfill for me; your love, O LORD, endures forever — do not abandon the works of your hands.

Psalm 138:8

Children's children are a crown to the aged, and parents are the pride of their children.

Proverbs 17:6

Discipline your son, and he will give you peace; he will bring delight to your soul.

Proverbs 29:17

So do not fear, for I am with you; do not be dismayed, for I am your God. I will strengthen you and help you; I will uphold you with my righteous right hand.

Isaiah 41:10

All your sons will be taught by the LORD, and great will be your children's peace.

Isaiah 54:13

He will turn the hearts of the fathers to their children, and the hearts of the children to their fathers; or else I will come and strike the land with a curse.

Malachi 4:6

We live by faith, not by sight.

2 Corinthians 5:7

Fathers, do not exasperate your children; instead, bring them up in the training and instruction of the Lord.

Ephesians 6:4

Let us hold unswervingly to the hope we profess, for he who promised is faithful.

Hebrews 10:23

Now faith is being sure of what we hope for and certain of what we do not see.

And without faith it is impossible to please God, because anyone who comes to him must believe that he exists and that he rewards those who earnestly seek him.

Hebrews 11:1,6

These have come so that your faith — of greater worth than gold, which perishes even though refined by fire — may be proved genuine and may result in praise, glory and honor when Jesus Christ is revealed.

1 Peter 1:7

But you are a chosen people, a royal priesthood, a holy nation, a people belonging to God, that you may declare the praises of him who called you out of darkness into his wonderful light.

1 Peter 2:9

Cast all your anxiety on him because he cares for you.

1 Peter 5:7

When Your Child Becomes Lazy and Disinterested

As for me, far be it from me that I should sin against the LORD by failing to pray for you. And I will teach you the way that is good and right.

1 Samuel 12:23

Now there were four men with leprosy at the entrance of the city gate. They said to each other, ''Why stay here until we die?

If we say, 'We'll go into the city' — the famine is there, and we will die. And if we stay here, we will die. So let's go over to the camp of the Arameans and surrender. If they spare us, we live; if they kill us, then we die.''

2 Kings 7:3,4

I will instruct you and teach you in the way you should go; I will counsel you and watch over you.

Psalm 32:8

Why are you downcast, O my soul? Why so disturbed within me? Put your hope in God, for I will yet praise him, my Savior and my God.

Psalm 43:5

Blessed is he whose help is the God of Jacob, whose hope is in the LORD his God.

Psalm 146:5

Let the wise listen and add to their learning, and let the discerning get guidance.

Proverbs 1:5

Hope deferred makes the heart sick, but a longing fulfilled is a tree of life.

Proverbs 13:12

The sluggard craves and gets nothing, but the desires of the diligent are fully satisfied.

Proverbs 13:4

Whatever your hand finds to do, do it with all your might, for in the grave, where you are going, there is neither working nor planning nor knowledge nor wisdom.

Ecclesiastes 9:10

If a man is lazy, the rafters sag; if his hands are idle, the house leaks.

Ecclesiastes 10:18

When the king heard this, he was greatly distressed; he was determined to rescue Daniel and made every effort until sundown to save him.

Daniel 6:14

In the same way, let your light shine before men, that they may see your good deeds and praise your Father in heaven.

Matthew 5:16

May the God of hope fill you with all joy and peace as you trust in him, so that you may overflow with hope by the power of the Holy Spirit.

Romans 15:13

Put on the full armor of God so that you can take your stand against the devil's schemes.

Therefore put on the full armor of God, so that when the day of evil comes, you may be able to stand your ground, and after you have done everything, to stand.

And pray in the Spirit on all occasions with all kinds of prayers and requests. With this in mind, be alert and always keep on praying for all the saints.

Ephesians 6:11,13,18

And the peace of God, which transcends all understanding, will guard your hearts and your minds in Christ Jesus.

Philippians 4:7

Whatever you do, work at it with all your heart, as working for the Lord, not for men.

Colossians 3:23

Be wise in the way you act toward outsiders; make the most of every opportunity.

Colossians 4:5

When Your Child Begins To Withdraw From You

I sought the LORD, and he answered me; he delivered me from all my fears.

Psalm 34:4

Be still, and know that I am God; I will be exalted among the nations, I will be exalted in the earth.

Psalm 46:10

He will not let your foot slip — he who watches over you will not slumber.
Psalm 121:3

For I was hungry and you gave me something to eat, I was thirsty and you gave me something to drink, I was a stranger and you invited me in, I needed clothes and you clothed me, I was sick and you looked after me, I was in prison and you came to visit me.

Then the righteous will answer him, "Lord, when did we see you hungry and feed you, or thirsty and give you something to drink?

When did we see you a stranger and invite you in, or needing clothes and clothe you?

When did we see you sick or in prison and go to visit you?"

The King will reply, "I tell you the truth, whatever you did for one of the least of these brothers of mine, you did for me."
Matthew 25:35-40

By standing firm you will gain life.
Luke 21:19

I will not leave you as orphans; I will come to you.

John 14:18

Not only so, but we also rejoice in our sufferings, because we know that suffering produces perseverance; perseverance, character; and character, hope.

And hope does not disappoint us, because God has poured out his love into our hearts by the Holy Spirit, whom he has given us.

Romans 5:3-5

Carry each other's burdens, and in this way you will fulfill the law of Christ.

Galatians 6:2

God is not unjust; he will not forget your work and the love you have shown him as you have helped his people and continue to help them.

Hebrews 6:10

If you really keep the royal law found in Scripture, "Love your neighbor as yourself," you are doing right.

James 2:8

If anyone has material possessions and sees his brother in need but has no pity on him, how can the love of God be in him?

Dear children, let us not love with words or tongue but with actions and in truth.

1 John 3:17,18

When Your Child Encounters Peer Pressure

The LORD is a refuge for the oppressed, a stronghold in times of trouble.

Psalm 9:9

I love you, O LORD, my strength.

The LORD is my rock, my fortress and my deliverer; my God is my rock, in whom I take refuge. He is my shield and the horn of my salvation, my stronghold.

Psalm 18:1,2

My flesh and my heart may fail, but God is the strength of my heart and my portion forever.

Psalm 73:26

A thousand may fall at your side, ten thousand at your right hand, but it will not come near you.

If you make the Most High your dwelling — even the LORD, who is my refuge — then no harm will befall you, no disaster will come near your tent.

Psalm 91:7,9,10

Praise the LORD, O my soul, and forget not all his benefits — who satisfies your desires with good things so that your youth is renewed like the eagle's.

Psalm 103:2,5

He sent forth his word and healed them; he rescued them from the grave.

Psalm 107:20

May there be peace within your walls and security within your citadels.

Psalm 122:7

In vain you rise early and stay up late, toiling for food to eat — for he grants sleep to those he loves.

Psalm 127:2

When you lie down, you will not be afraid;
when you lie down, your sleep will be sweet.
Proverbs 3:24

Wicked men are overthrown and are no more, but the house of the righteous stands firm.
Proverbs 12:7

But those who hope in the LORD will renew their strength. They will soar on wings like eagles; they will run and not grow weary, they will walk and not be faint.
Isaiah 40:31

Surely he took up our infirmities and carried our sorrows, yet we considered him stricken by God, smitten by him, and afflicted.
Isaiah 53:4

I tell you the truth, whatever you bind on earth will be bound in heaven, and whatever you loose on earth will be loosed in heaven.
Matthew 18:18

Do not let your hearts be troubled. Trust in God; trust also in me.

Peace I leave with you; my peace I give you. I do not give to you as the world gives. Do not let your hearts be troubled and do not be afraid.

John 14:1,27

Do not be anxious about anything, but in everything, by prayer and petition, with thanksgiving, present your requests to God.

And the peace of God, which transcends all understanding, will guard your hearts and your minds in Christ Jesus.

Philippians 4:6,7

Cast all your anxiety on him because he cares for you.

1 Peter 5:7

When Your Child Is Jealous of Your Attention Shown to Others

I will praise the LORD, who counsels me; even at night my heart instructs me.

I have set the LORD always before me. Because he is at my right hand, I will not be shaken.

Therefore my heart is glad and my tongue rejoices; my body also will rest secure.

Psalm 16:7-9

Surely you desire truth in the inner parts; you teach me wisdom in the inmost place.

Create in me a pure heart, O God, and renew a steadfast spirit within me.

Psalm 51:6,10

In God, whose word I praise, in God I trust; I will not be afraid. What can mortal man do to me?

Psalm 56:4

Teach me your way, O LORD, and I will walk in your truth; give me an undivided heart, that I may fear your name.

Psalm 86:11

Trust in the LORD with all your heart and lean not on your own understanding; in all your ways acknowledge him, and he will make your paths straight.

For the LORD will be your confidence.

Proverbs 3:5,6,26a

Fear of man will prove to be a snare, but whoever trusts in the LORD is kept safe.

Proverbs 29:25

Surely God is my salvation; I will trust and not be afraid. The LORD, the LORD, is my strength and my song; he has become my salvation.

Isaiah 12:2

Love is patient, love is kind. It does not envy, it does not boast, it is not proud.

It is not rude, it is not self-seeking, it is not easily angered, it keeps no record of wrongs.

1 Corinthians 13:4,5

The weapons we fight with are not the weapons of the world. On the contrary, they have divine power to demolish strongholds.

2 Corinthians 10:4

Finally, be strong in the Lord and in his mighty power.

Ephesians 6:10

Finally, brothers, whatever is true, whatever is noble, whatever is right, whatever is pure, whatever is lovely, whatever is admirable — if anything is excellent or praiseworthy — think about such things.
Philippians 4:8

If any of you lacks wisdom, he should ask God, who gives generously to all without finding fault, and it will be given to him.
James 1:5

Dear friends, do not be surprised at the painful trial you are suffering, as though something strange were happening to you.
1 Peter 4:12

When Your Child Acquires a Poor Self-Image

Then God said, "Let us make man in our image, in our likeness, and let them rule over the fish of the sea and the birds of the air, over the livestock, over all the earth, and over all the creatures that move along the ground."

So God created man in his own image, in the image of God he created him; male and female he created them.

Genesis 1:26,27

You deserted the Rock, who fathered you; you forgot the God who gave you birth.

Deuteronomy 32:18

"The LORD who delivered me from the paw of the lion and the paw of the bear will deliver me from the hand of this Philistine."
Saul said to David, "Go, and the LORD be with you."

1 Samuel 17:37

But you are a shield around me, O LORD; you bestow glory on me and lift up my head.

Psalm 3:3

I will not fear the tens of thousands drawn up against me on every side.

Psalm 3:6

The LORD is my light and my salvation — whom shall I fear? The LORD is the stronghold of my life — of whom shall I be afraid?

Though an army besiege me, my heart will not fear; though war break out against me, even then will I be confident.

For in the day of trouble he will keep me safe in his dwelling; he will hide me in the shelter of his tabernacle and set me high upon a rock.

Psalm 27:1,3,5

It is better to take refuge in the LORD than to trust in man.

Psalm 118:8

I have hidden your word in my heart that I might not sin against you.

Psalm 119:11

For the LORD will be your confidence and will keep your foot from being snared.

Proverbs 3:26

He who fears the LORD has a secure fortress, and for his children it will be a refuge.

Proverbs 14:26

But now, this is what the LORD says — he who created you, O Jacob, he who formed you, O Israel: "Fear not, for I have redeemed you; I have summoned you by name; you are mine.

Everyone who is called by my name, whom I created for my glory, whom I formed and made.

The people I formed for myself that they may proclaim my praise."

Isaiah 43:1,7,21

This is what the LORD says — your Redeemer, who formed you in the womb: I am the LORD, who has made all things, who alone stretched out the heavens, who spread out the earth by myself.

Isaiah 44:24

Before I formed you in the womb I knew you, before you were born I set you apart; I appointed you as a prophet to the nations.

Jeremiah 1:5

You did not choose me, but I chose you and appointed you to go and bear fruit — fruit that will last. Then the Father will give you whatever you ask in my name.

John 15:16

And exchanged the glory of the immortal God for images made to look like mortal man and birds and animals and reptiles.

Romans 1:23

"For who has known the mind of the Lord that he may instruct him?" But we have the mind of Christ.

1 Corinthians 2:16

The god of this age has blinded the minds of unbelievers, so that they cannot see the light of the gospel of the glory of Christ, who is the image of God.

2 Corinthians 4:4

Being confident of this, that he who began a good work in you will carry it on to completion until the day of Christ Jesus.

Philippians 1:6

Do nothing out of selfish ambition or vain conceit, but in humility consider others better than yourselves.

Each of you should look not only to your own interests, but also to the interests of others.

Your attitude should be the same as that of Christ Jesus.

Philippians 2:3-5

He is the image of the invisible God, the firstborn over all creation.

Colossians 1:15

And have put on the new self, which is being renewed in knowledge in the image of its Creator.

Colossians 3:10

You, dear children, are from God and have overcome them, because the one who is in you is greater than the one who is in the world.

They are from the world and therefore speak from the viewpoint of the world, and the world listens to them.

We are from God, and whoever knows God listens to us; but whoever is not from God does not listen to us. This is how we recognize the Spirit of truth and the spirit of falsehood.

1 John 4:4-6

When Your Child Becomes Unforgiving Toward You

Commit your way to the LORD; trust in him and he will do this:

He will make your righteousness shine like the dawn, the justice of your cause like the noonday sun.

Psalm 37:5,6

Commit to the LORD whatever you do, and your plans will succeed.

Proverbs 16:3

Blessed are the peacemakers, for they will be called sons of God.

Matthew 5:9

Forgive us our debts, as we also have forgiven our debtors.

And lead us not into temptation, but deliver us from the evil one.

For if you forgive men when they sin against you, your heavenly Father will also forgive you.

But if you do not forgive men their sins, your Father will not forgive your sins.

Matthew 6:12-15

Do not judge, and you will not be judged. Do not condemn, and you will not be condemned. Forgive, and you will be forgiven.

Luke 6:37

Jesus said, "Father, forgive them, for they do not know what they are doing." And they divided up his clothes by casting lots.

Luke 23:34

Love is patient, love is kind. It does not envy, it does not boast, it is not proud.

1 Corinthians 13:4

If you forgive anyone, I also forgive him. And what I have forgiven — if there was anything to forgive — I have forgiven in the sight of Christ for your sake, in order that Satan might not outwit us. For we are not unaware of his schemes.

2 Corinthians 2:10,11

We demolish arguments and every pretension that sets itself up against the knowledge of God, and we take captive every thought to make it obedient to Christ.

2 Corinthians 10:5

Therefore each of you must put off falsehood and speak truthfully to his neighbor, for we are all members of one body.

"In your anger do not sin": Do not let the sun go down while you are still angry, and do not give the devil a foothold.

Be kind and compassionate to one another, forgiving each other, just as in Christ God forgave you.

Ephesians 4:25-27,32

Finally, brothers, whatever is true, whatever is noble, whatever is right, whatever is pure, whatever is lovely, whatever is admirable — if anything is excellent or praiseworthy — think about such things.

I know what it is to be in need, and I know what it is to have plenty. I have learned the secret of being content in any and every situation, whether well fed or hungry, whether living in plenty or in want.

I can do everything through him who gives me strength.

And my God will meet all your needs according to his glorious riches in Christ Jesus.
Philippians 4:8,12,13,19

For we know him who said, "It is mine to avenge; I will repay," and again, "The Lord will judge his people."
Hebrews 10:30

Bear with each other and forgive whatever grievances you may have against one another. Forgive as the Lord forgave you.

And over all these virtues put on love, which binds them all together in perfect unity.
Colossians 3:13,14

If any of you lacks wisdom, he should ask God, who gives generously to all without finding fault, and it will be given to him.

James 1:5

But if you harbor bitter envy and selfish ambition in your hearts, do not boast about it or deny the truth.

For where you have envy and selfish ambition, there you find disorder and every evil practice.

But the wisdom that comes from heaven is first of all pure; then peace-loving, considerate, submissive, full of mercy and good fruit, impartial and sincere.

Peacemakers who sow in peace raise a harvest of righteousness.

James 3:14,16-18

Therefore confess your sins to each other and pray for each other so that you may be healed. The prayer of a righteous man is powerful and effective.

James 5:16

When Your Child Becomes Quarrelsome

But Samuel replied: "Does the LORD delight in burnt offerings and sacrifices as much as in obeying the voice of the LORD? To obey is better than sacrifice, and to heed is better than the fat of rams.

For rebellion is like the sin of divination, and arrogance like the evil of idolatry. Because you have rejected the word of the LORD, he has rejected you as king."

1 Samuel 15:22,23

A man's wisdom gives him patience; it is to his glory to overlook an offense.

Proverbs 19:11

It is to a man's honor to avoid strife, but every fool is quick to quarrel.

Proverbs 20:3

If a ruler's anger rises against you, do not leave your post; calmness can lay great errors to rest.

Ecclesiastes 10:4

"If you are willing and obedient, you will eat the best from the land; but if you resist and rebel, you will be devoured by the sword." For the mouth of the LORD has spoken.

Isaiah 1:19,20

Blessed are the peacemakers, for they will be called sons of God.

Matthew 5:9

If it is possible, as far as it depends on you, live at peace with everyone.

Romans 12:18

Love is patient, love is kind. It does not envy, it does not boast, it is not proud.

It is not rude, it is not self-seeking, it is not easily angered, it keeps no record of wrongs.

Love does not delight in evil but rejoices with the truth.

It always protects, always trusts, always hopes, always perseveres.

1 Corinthians 13:4-7

And we urge you, brothers, warn those who are idle.

1 Thessalonians 5:14a

And the Lord's servant must not quarrel; instead, he must be kind to everyone, able to teach, not resentful.

2 Timothy 2:24

To slander no one, to be peaceable and considerate, and to show true humility toward all men.

Titus 3:2

Make every effort to live in peace with all men and to be holy; without holiness no one will see the Lord.

Hebrews 12:14

Peacemakers who sow in peace raise a harvest of righteousness.

James 3:18

Young men, in the same way be submissive to those who are older. All of you, clothe yourselves with humility toward one another, because, ''God opposes the proud but gives grace to the humble.''

Humble yourselves, therefore, under God's mighty hand, that he may lift you up in due time.

1 Peter 5:5,6

When Your Child Must Cope With Parental Disharmony

Since you are my rock and my fortress, for the sake of your name lead and guide me.

Free me from the trap that is set for me, for you are my refuge.

Into your hands I commit my spirit; redeem me, O LORD, the God of truth.

Psalm 31:3-5

You are my hiding place; you will protect me from trouble and surround me with songs of deliverance. Selah.

Psalm 32:7

Commit your way to the LORD; trust in him and he will do this:

He will make your righteousness shine like the dawn, the justice of your cause like the noonday sun.

Be still before the LORD and wait patiently for him; do not fret when men succeed in their ways, when they carry out their wicked schemes.

Psalm 37:5-7

I wait for you, O LORD; you will answer, O Lord my God.

Psalm 38:15

I call on the LORD in my distress, and he answers me.

Save me, O LORD, from lying lips and from deceitful tongues.

Psalm 120:1,2

Though I walk in the midst of trouble, you preserve my life; you stretch out your hand against the anger of my foes, with your right hand you save me.

Psalm 138:7

There are six things the LORD hates, seven that are detestable to him: haughty eyes, a lying tongue, hands that shed innocent blood, a heart that devises wicked schemes, feet that are quick to rush into evil, a false witness who pours out lies and a man who stirs up dissension among brothers.

Proverbs 6:16-19

Commit to the LORD whatever you do,
and your plans will succeed.

Proverbs 16:3

Do not say, "I'll do to him as he has done
to me; I'll pay that man back for what he did."

Proverbs 24:29

When you pass through the waters, I will
be with you; and when you pass through the
rivers, they will not sweep over you. When
you walk through the fire, you will not be
burned; the flames will not set you ablaze.

Isaiah 43:2

The LORD will guide you always; he will
satisfy your needs in a sun-scorched land and
will strengthen your frame. You will be like
a well-watered garden, like a spring whose
waters never fail.

Isaiah 58:11

I the LORD search the heart and examine
the mind, to reward a man according to his
conduct, according to what his deeds deserve.

Jeremiah 17:10

The LORD is good, a refuge in times of trouble. He cares for those who trust in him.

Nahum 1:7

And when you stand praying, if you hold anything against anyone, forgive him, so that your Father in heaven may forgive you your sins.

Mark 11:25

Who is going to harm you if you are eager to do good?

1 Peter 3:13

Cast all your anxiety on him because he cares for you.

1 Peter 5:7

When Your Child Becomes Sick

The LORD will keep you free from every disease. He will not inflict on you the horrible diseases you knew in Egypt, but he will inflict them on all who hate you.

Deuteronomy 7:15

Praise the LORD, O my soul, and forget not all his benefits — who forgives all your sins and heals all your diseases.

Psalm 103:2,3

My son, pay attention to what I say; listen closely to my words.

Do not let them out of your sight, keep them within your heart; for they are life to those who find them and health to a man's whole body.

Proverbs 4:20-22

Surely he took up our infirmities and carried our sorrows, yet we considered him stricken by God, smitten by him, and afflicted.

But he was pierced for our transgressions, he was crushed for our iniquities; the punishment that brought us peace was upon him, and by his wounds we are healed.

Isaiah 53:4,5

Heal me, O LORD, and I will be healed; save me and I will be saved, for you are the one I praise.

Jeremiah 17:14

"But I will restore you to health and heal your wounds," declares the LORD.

Jeremiah 30:17a

Jesus said to him, "I will go and heal him."

Matthew 8:7

Jesus Christ is the same yesterday and today and forever.

Hebrews 13:8

Is any one of you in trouble? He should pray. Is anyone happy? Let him sing songs of praise.

Is any one of you sick? He should call the elders of the church to pray over him and anoint him with oil in the name of the Lord.

And the prayer offered in faith will make the sick person well; the Lord will raise him up. If he has sinned, he will be forgiven.

Therefore confess your sins to each other and pray for each other so that you may be healed. The prayer of a righteous man is powerful and effective.

James 5:13-16

Dear friend, I pray that you may enjoy good health and that all may go well with you, even as your soul is getting along well.

3 John 1:2

When Your Child Has Thoughts of Suicide

So God created man in his own image, in the image of God he created him; male and female he created them.

Genesis 1:27

You deserted the Rock, who fathered you; you forgot the God who gave you birth.

Deuteronomy 32:18

One of you routs a thousand, because the LORD your God fights for you, just as he promised.

Joshua 23:10

He will guard the feet of his saints, but the wicked will be silenced in darkness. It is not by strength that one prevails.

1 Samuel 2:9

"The LORD who delivered me from the paw of the lion and the paw of the bear will deliver me from the hand of this Philistine." Saul said to David, "Go, and the LORD be with you."

1 Samuel 17:37

But you are a shield around me, O LORD; you bestow glory on me and lift up my head.

Psalm 3:3

I will not fear the tens of thousands drawn up against me on every side.

Psalm 3:6

The LORD is my light and my salvation — whom shall I fear? The LORD is the stronghold of my life — of whom shall I be afraid?

Though an army besiege me, my heart will not fear; though war break out against me, even then will I be confident.

For in the day of trouble he will keep me safe in his dwelling; he will hide me in the shelter of his tabernacle and set me high upon a rock.

Psalm 27:1,3,5

It is better to take refuge in the LORD than to trust in man.

Psalm 118:8

I have hidden your word in my heart that I might not sin against you.

Psalm 119:11

For the LORD will be your confidence and will keep your foot from being snared.

Proverbs 3:26

He who fears the LORD has a secure fortress, and for his children it will be a refuge.

Proverbs 14:26

But now, this is what the LORD says — he who created you, O Jacob, he who formed you, O Israel: ''Fear not, for I have redeemed you; I have summoned you by name; you are mine.

Everyone who is called by my name, whom I created for my glory, whom I formed and made.

The people I formed for myself that they may proclaim my praise.''

Isaiah 43:1,7,21

This is what the LORD says — your Redeemer, who formed you in the womb: I am the LORD, who has made all things, who alone stretched out the heavens, who spread out the earth by myself.

Isaiah 44:24

Before I formed you in the womb I knew you, before you were born I set you apart; I appointed you as a prophet to the nations.

Jeremiah 1:5

''For who has known the mind of the Lord that he may instruct him?'' But we have the mind of Christ.

1 Corinthians 2:16

The god of this age has blinded the minds of unbelievers, so that they cannot see the light of the gospel of the glory of Christ, who is the image of God.

2 Corinthians 4:4

Being confident of this, that he who began a good work in you will carry it on to completion until the day of Christ Jesus.

Philippians 1:6

Each of you should look not only to your own interests, but also to the interests of others.

Your attitude should be the same as that of Christ Jesus.

Philippians 2:4,5

And have put on the new self, which is being renewed in knowledge in the image of its Creator.

Colossians 3:10

You, dear children, are from God and have overcome them, because the one who is in you is greater than the one who is in the world.

They are from the world and therefore speak from the viewpoint of the world, and the world listens to them.

We are from God, and whoever knows God listens to us; but whoever is not from God does not listen to us. This is how we recognize the Spirit of truth and the spirit of falsehood.

1 John 4:4-6

When Your Child
Does Not Want To Attend Church

Only be careful, and watch yourselves closely so that you do not forget the things your eyes have seen or let them slip from your heart as long as you live. Teach them to your children and to their children after them.

Deuteronomy 4:9

These commandments that I give you today are to be upon your hearts.

Impress them on your children. Talk about them when you sit at home and when you walk along the road, when you lie down and when you get up.

Deuteronomy 6:6,7

Teach them to your children, talking about them when you sit at home and when you walk along the road, when you lie down and when you get up.

Deuteronomy 11:19

He decreed statutes for Jacob and established the law in Israel, which he commanded our forefathers to teach their children, so the next generation would know them, even the children yet to be born, and they in turn would tell their children.

Then they would put their trust in God and would not forget his deeds but would keep his commands.

Psalm 78:5-7

A good man leaves an inheritance for his children's children, but a sinner's wealth is stored up for the righteous.

Proverbs 13:22

The righteous man leads a blameless life; blessed are his children after him.

Proverbs 20:7

Train a child in the way he should go, and when he is old he will not turn from it.

Proverbs 22:6

By wisdom a house is built, and through understanding it is established.

Proverbs 24:3

Discipline your son, and he will give you peace; he will bring delight to your soul.

Proverbs 29:17

Tell it to your children, and let your children tell it to their children, and their children to the next generation.

Joel 1:3

But seek first his kingdom and his righteousness, and all these things will be given to you as well.

Matthew 6:33

Fathers, do not exasperate your children; instead, bring them up in the training and instruction of the Lord.

Ephesians 6:4

If anyone does not provide for his relatives, and especially for his immediate family, he has denied the faith and is worse than an unbeliever.

1 Timothy 5:8

When Your Child Is Heartbroken by Divorce

For the LORD your God is a merciful God; he will not abandon or destroy you or forget the covenant with your forefathers, which he confirmed to them by oath.

Deuteronomy 4:31

Be strong and courageous. Do not be afraid or terrified because of them, for the LORD your God goes with you; he will never leave you nor forsake you.

Deuteronomy 31:6

For the sake of his great name the LORD will not reject his people, because the LORD was pleased to make you his own.

1 Samuel 12:22

Those who know your name will trust in you, for you, LORD, have never forsaken those who seek you.

Psalm 9:10

Though my father and mother forsake me, the LORD will receive me.
Teach me your way, O LORD; lead me in a straight path because of my oppressors.

Psalm 27:10,11

I was young and now I am old, yet I have never seen the righteous forsaken or their children begging bread.

Psalm 37:25

Why are you downcast, O my soul? Why so disturbed within me? Put your hope in God, for I will yet praise him, my Savior and my God.

Psalm 43:5

"Because he loves me," says the LORD, "I will rescue him; I will protect him, for he acknowledges my name.

He will call upon me, and I will answer him; I will be with him in trouble, I will deliver him and honor him."

Psalm 91:14,15

For the LORD will not reject his people; he will never forsake his inheritance.

Psalm 94:14

The poor and needy search for water, but there is none; their tongues are parched with thirst. But I the LORD will answer them; I, the God of Israel, will not forsake them.

Isaiah 41:17

Can a mother forget the baby at her breast and have no compassion on the child she has borne? Though she may forget, I will not forget you!

See, I have engraved you on the palms of my hands; your walls are ever before me.

Isaiah 49:15,16

No longer will they call you Deserted, or name your land Desolate. But you will be called Hephzibah, and your land Beulah; for the LORD will take delight in you, and your land will be married.

Isaiah 62:4

The Spirit of the Lord is on me, because he has anointed me to preach good news to the poor. He has sent me to proclaim freedom for the prisoners and recovery of sight for the blind, to release the oppressed, to proclaim the year of the Lord's favor.

Luke 4:18,19

Persecuted, but not abandoned; struck down, but not destroyed.

2 Corinthians 4:9

Cast all your anxiety on him because he cares for you.

1 Peter 5:7

When Your Child Is Beyond Your Daily Influence

The LORD turn his face toward you and give you peace.

Numbers 6:26

For the LORD your God is a merciful God; he will not abandon or destroy you or forget the covenant with your forefathers, which he confirmed to them by oath.

Deuteronomy 4:31

Be strong and courageous. Do not be afraid or terrified because of them, for the LORD your God goes with you; he will never leave you nor forsake you.

The LORD himself goes before you and will be with you; he will never leave you nor forsake you. Do not be afraid; do not be discouraged.

Deuteronomy 31:6,8

Wait for the LORD; be strong and take heart and wait for the LORD.

Psalm 27:14

Delight yourself in the LORD and he will give you the desires of your heart.

I was young and now I am old, yet I have never seen the righteous forsaken or their children begging bread.

Psalm 37:4,25

Sons are a heritage from the LORD, children a reward from him.

Like arrows in the hands of a warrior are sons born in one's youth.

Blessed is the man whose quiver is full of them. They will not be put to shame.

Psalm 127:3-5a

In his heart a man plans his course, but the LORD determines his steps.

Proverbs 16:9

Train a child in the way he should go, and when he is old he will not turn from it.

Proverbs 22:6

The father of a righteous man has great joy; he who has a wise son delights in him.

Proverbs 23:24

Discipline your son, and he will give you peace; he will bring delight to your soul.

Proverbs 29:17

Can a mother forget the baby at her breast and have no compassion on the child she has borne? Though she may forget, I will not forget you!

See, I have engraved you on the palms of my hands; your walls are ever before me.

Isaiah 49:15,16

And teaching them to obey everything I have commanded you. And surely I am with you always, to the very end of the age.

Matthew 28:20

These have come so that your faith — of greater worth than gold, which perishes even though refined by fire — may be proved genuine and may result in praise, glory and honor when Jesus Christ is revealed.

1 Peter 1:7

Cast all your anxiety on him because he cares for you.

1 Peter 5:7

When You Have Made Mistakes in Raising Your Child

Then the LORD your God will restore your fortunes and have compassion on you and gather you again from all the nations where he scattered you.

Deuteronomy 30:3

If my people, who are called by my name, will humble themselves and pray and seek my face and turn from their wicked ways, then will I hear from heaven and will forgive their sin and will heal their land.

2 Chronicles 7:14

Teach me what I cannot see; if I have done wrong, I will not do so again.

Job 34:32

He restores my soul. He guides me in paths of righteousness for his name's sake.

Psalm 23:3

Wait for the LORD; be strong and take heart and wait for the LORD.

Psalm 27:14

We wait in hope for the LORD; he is our help and our shield.

Psalm 33:20

Create in me a pure heart, O God, and renew a steadfast spirit within me.

Do not cast me from your presence or take your Holy Spirit from me.

Restore to me the joy of your salvation and grant me a willing spirit, to sustain me.

Psalm 51:10-12

Cast your cares on the LORD and he will sustain you; he will never let the righteous fall.

Psalm 55:22

I wait for the LORD, my soul waits, and in his word I put my hope.

Psalm 130:5

The LORD will fulfill for me; your love, O LORD, endures forever — do not abandon the works of your hands.

Psalm 138:8

So do not fear, for I am with you; do not be dismayed, for I am your God. I will strengthen you and help you; I will uphold you with my righteous right hand.

Isaiah 41:10

For I will pour water on the thirsty land, and streams on the dry ground; I will pour out my Spirit on your offspring, and my blessing on your descendants.

Isaiah 44:3

I will repay you for the years the locusts have eaten — the great locust and the young locust, the other locusts and the locust swarm — my great army that I sent among you.

Joel 2:25

He replied, ''Because you have so little faith. I tell you the truth, if you have faith as small as a mustard seed, you can say to this mountain, 'Move from here to there' and it will move. Nothing will be impossible for you.''

Matthew 17:20

They replied, ''Believe in the Lord Jesus, and you will be saved — you and your household.''

Acts 16:31

Paul looked straight at the Sanhedrin and said, "My brothers, I have fulfilled my duty to God in all good conscience to this day."

Acts 23:1

And we know that in all things God works for the good of those who love him, who have been called according to his purpose.

Romans 8:28

But you are a chosen people, a royal priesthood, a holy nation, a people belonging to God, that you may declare the praises of him who called you out of darkness into his wonderful light.

1 Peter 2:9

Cast all your anxiety on him because he cares for you.

1 Peter 5:7

When Your Child Seems Unappreciative

But some troublemakers said, "How can this fellow save us?" They despised him and brought him no gifts. But Saul kept silent.

1 Samuel 10:27

He restores my soul. He guides me in paths of righteousness for his name's sake.

Psalm 23:3

Hide me from the conspiracy of the wicked, from that noisy crowd of evildoers.

Psalm 64:2

The end of a matter is better than its beginning, and patience is better than pride.

Do not be quickly provoked in your spirit, for anger resides in the lap of fools.

Ecclesiastes 7:8,9

Blessed are those who are persecuted because of righteousness, for theirs is the kingdom of heaven.

Blessed are you when people insult you, persecute you and falsely say all kinds of evil against you because of me.

Rejoice and be glad, because great is your reward in heaven, for in the same way they persecuted the prophets who were before you.

Matthew 5:10-12

Then Peter came to Jesus and asked, "Lord, how many times shall I forgive my brother when he sins against me? Up to seven times?"

Jesus answered, "I tell you, not seven times, but seventy-seven times."

Matthew 18:21,22

And when you stand praying, if you hold anything against anyone, forgive him, so that your Father in heaven may forgive you your sins.

Mark 11:25

So watch yourselves. If your brother sins, rebuke him, and if he repents, forgive him.

Luke 17:3

Do not be overcome by evil, but overcome evil with good.

Romans 12:21

Anyone who does wrong will be repaid for his wrong, and there is no favoritism.

Colossians 3:25

For we know him who said, "It is mine to avenge; I will repay," and again, "The Lord will judge his people."

Hebrews 10:30

So we say with confidence, "The Lord is my helper; I will not be afraid. What can man do to me?"

Hebrews 13:6

Get rid of all bitterness, rage and anger, brawling and slander, along with every form of malice.

Be kind and compassionate to one another, forgiving each other, just as in Christ God forgave you.

Ephesians 4:31,32

But how is it to your credit if you receive a beating for doing wrong and endure it? But if you suffer for doing good and you endure it, this is commendable before God.

1 Peter 2:20

Do not repay evil with evil or insult with insult, but with blessing, because to this you were called so that you may inherit a blessing.

For, "Whoever would love life and see good days must keep his tongue from evil and his lips from deceitful speech."

1 Peter 3:9,10

Dear friends, do not be surprised at the painful trial you are suffering, as though something strange were happening to you.

But rejoice that you participate in the sufferings of Christ, so that you may be overjoyed when his glory is revealed.

If you are insulted because of the name of Christ, you are blessed, for the Spirit of glory and of God rests on you.

1 Peter 4:12-14

When Your Child Seems Irresponsible

Be strong and courageous. Do not be afraid or terrified because of them, for the LORD your God goes with you; he will never leave you nor forsake you.

Deuteronomy 31:6

Wait for the LORD; be strong and take heart and wait for the LORD.

Psalm 27:14

I have hidden your word in my heart that I might not sin against you.

Psalm 119:11

When you walk, they will guide you; when you sleep, they will watch over you; when you awake, they will speak to you.

For these commands are a lamp, this teaching is a light, and the corrections of discipline are the way to life.

Proverbs 6:22,23

A patient man has great understanding, but a quick-tempered man displays folly.

Proverbs 14:29

The tongue that brings healing is a tree of life, but a deceitful tongue crushes the spirit.

Proverbs 15:4

Better to be lowly in spirit and among the oppressed than to share plunder with the proud.

Whoever gives heed to instruction prospers, and blessed is he who trusts in the LORD.

The wise in heart are called discerning, and pleasant words promote instruction.

Proverbs 16:19-21

Starting a quarrel is like breaching a dam; so drop the matter before a dispute breaks out.

A man of knowledge uses words with restraint, and a man of understanding is even-tempered.

Proverbs 17:14,27

The end of a matter is better than its beginning, and patience is better than pride.

Ecclesiastes 7:8

The Spirit of the LORD will rest on him — the Spirit of wisdom and of understanding, the Spirit of counsel and of power, the Spirit of knowledge and of the fear of the LORD.

Isaiah 11:2

But they could not stand up against his wisdom or the Spirit by whom he spoke.

Acts 6:10

Never be lacking in zeal, but keep your spiritual fervor, serving the Lord.

If it is possible, as far as it depends on you, live at peace with everyone.

Romans 12:11,18

For God did not give us a spirit of timidity, but a spirit of power, of love and of self-discipline.

2 Timothy 1:7

If any of you lacks wisdom, he should ask God, who gives generously to all without finding fault, and it will be given to him.

James 1:5

But the wisdom that comes from heaven is first of all pure; then peace-loving, considerate, submissive, full of mercy and good fruit, impartial and sincere.

James 3:17

When Your Child Is Not Committed to God

The eternal God is your refuge, and underneath are the everlasting arms. He will drive out your enemy before you, saying, "Destroy him!"

Deuteronomy 33:27

If the LORD delights in a man's way, he makes his steps firm.

Psalm 37:23

Be still, and know that I am God; I will be exalted among the nations, I will be exalted in the earth.

Psalm 46:10

And call upon me in the day of trouble;
I will deliver you, and you will honor me.
Psalm 50:15

Cast your cares on the LORD and he will
sustain you; he will never let the righteous fall.
Psalm 55:22

My flesh and my heart may fail, but God
is the strength of my heart and my portion
forever.
Psalm 73:26

When anxiety was great within me, your
consolation brought joy to my soul.
Psalm 94:19

He heals the brokenhearted and binds up
their wounds.
Psalm 147:3

So do not fear, for I am with you; do not
be dismayed, for I am your God. I will
strengthen you and help you; I will uphold you
with my righteous right hand.
All who rage against you will surely be
ashamed and disgraced; those who oppose you
will be as nothing and perish.

Though you search for your enemies, you will not find them. Those who wage war against you will be as nothing at all.

For I am the LORD, your God, who takes hold of your right hand and says to you, Do not fear; I will help you.

Isaiah 41:10-13

I have not come to call the righteous, but sinners to repentance.

Luke 5:32

For the Son of Man came to seek and to save what was lost.

Luke 19:10

By standing firm you will gain life.

Luke 21:19

I am not saying this because I am in need, for I have learned to be content whatever the circumstances.

I know what it is to be in need, and I know what it is to have plenty. I have learned the secret of being content in any and every situation, whether well fed or hungry, whether living in plenty or in want.

I can do everything through him who gives me strength.

Philippians 4:11-13

Endure hardship with us like a good soldier of Christ Jesus.

2 Timothy 2:3

The Lord is not slow in keeping his promise, as some understand slowness. He is patient with you, not wanting anyone to perish, but everyone to come to repentance.

2 Peter 3:9

When You Fear the Consequences of His Lifestyle

I am still confident of this: I will see the goodness of the LORD in the land of the living.

Psalm 27:13

Commit your way to the LORD; trust in him and he will do this:

He will make your righteousness shine like the dawn, the justice of your cause like the noonday sun.

Psalm 37:5,6

Blessed are they who keep his statutes and seek him with all their heart.

Give me understanding, and I will keep your law and obey it with all my heart.

I have hidden your word in my heart that I might not sin against you.

Your word is a lamp to my feet and a light for my path.

Psalm 119:2,34,11,105

Trust in the LORD with all your heart and lean not on your own understanding.

Proverbs 3:5

Discipline your son, and he will give you peace; he will bring delight to your soul.

Proverbs 29:17

Because the Sovereign LORD helps me, I will not be disgraced. Therefore have I set my face like flint, and I know I will not be put to shame.

Isaiah 50:7

You will seek me and find me when you seek me with all your heart.

Jeremiah 29:13

I have given you authority to trample on snakes and scorpions and to overcome all the power of the enemy; nothing will harm you.

Luke 10:19

In the same way, any of you who does not give up everything he has cannot be my disciple.

Luke 14:33

Peace I leave with you; my peace I give you. I do not give to you as the world gives. Do not let your hearts be troubled and do not be afraid.

John 14:27

They replied, "Believe in the Lord Jesus, and you will be saved — you and your household."

Acts 16:31

Get rid of all bitterness, rage and anger, brawling and slander, along with every form of malice.

Be kind and compassionate to one another, forgiving each other, just as in Christ God forgave you.

Ephesians 4:31,32

Fathers, do not exasperate your children; instead, bring them up in the training and instruction of the Lord.

Ephesians 6:4

But whatever was to my profit I now consider loss for the sake of Christ.

Philippians 3:7

For God did not give us a spirit of timidity, but a spirit of power, of love and of self-discipline.

2 Timothy 1:7

There is no fear in love. But perfect love drives out fear, because fear has to do with punishment. The one who fears is not made perfect in love.

1 John 4:18

When Your Child Blames You for His Problems

I will praise the LORD, who counsels me; even at night my heart instructs me.

I have set the LORD always before me. Because he is at my right hand, I will not be shaken.

Psalm 16:7,8

A righteous man may have many troubles, but the LORD delivers him from them all.
Psalm 34:19

Cast your cares on the LORD and he will sustain you; he will never let the righteous fall.
Psalm 55:22

He alone is my rock and my salvation; he is my fortress, I will never be shaken.
Psalm 62:2

The LORD will fulfill for me; your love, O LORD, endures forever — do not abandon the works of your hands.
Psalm 138:8

Trust in the LORD with all your heart and lean not on your own understanding; in all your ways acknowledge him, and he will make your paths straight.
Proverbs 3:5,6

A gentle answer turns away wrath, but a harsh word stirs up anger.

The tongue of the wise commends knowledge, but the mouth of the fool gushes folly.

Proverbs 15:1,2

Whoever gives heed to instruction prospers, and blessed is he who trusts in the LORD.

Proverbs 16:20

Fear of man will prove to be a snare, but whoever trusts in the LORD is kept safe.

Proverbs 29:25

Surely God is my salvation; I will trust and not be afraid. The LORD, the LORD, is my strength and my song; he has become my salvation.

Isaiah 12:2

You will keep in perfect peace him whose mind is steadfast, because he trusts in you.

Trust in the LORD forever, for the LORD, the LORD, is the Rock eternal.

Isaiah 26:3,4

O LORD, be gracious to us; we long for you. Be our strength every morning, our salvation in time of distress.

Isaiah 33:2

So do not fear, for I am with you; do not be dismayed, for I am your God. I will strengthen you and help you; I will uphold you with my righteous right hand.

Isaiah 41:10

But as for me, I watch in hope for the LORD, I wait for God my Savior; my God will hear me.

Micah 7:7

What, then, shall we say in response to this? If God is for us, who can be against us?

Romans 8:31

"In your anger do not sin": Do not let the sun go down while you are still angry.

Get rid of all bitterness, rage and anger, brawling and slander, along with every form of malice.

Ephesians 4:26,31

See to it that no one misses the grace of God and that no bitter root grows up to cause trouble and defile many.

Hebrews 12:15

Dear friends, do not be surprised at the painful trial you are suffering, as though something strange were happening to you.

But rejoice that you participate in the sufferings of Christ, so that you may be overjoyed when his glory is revealed.

1 Peter 4:12,13

Your Wife

When Your Wife Seems Unsupportive of Your Dreams and Goals

The LORD is my light and my salvation — whom shall I fear? The LORD is the stronghold of my life — of whom shall I be afraid?

Though an army besiege me, my heart will not fear; though war break out against me, even then will I be confident.

Wait for the LORD; be strong and take heart and wait for the LORD.

Psalm 27:1,3,14

Since you are my rock and my fortress, for the sake of your name lead and guide me.

Free me from the trap that is set for me, for you are my refuge.

Psalm 31:3,4

You are my hiding place; you will protect me from trouble and surround me with songs of deliverance. Selah.

I will instruct you and teach you in the way you should go; I will counsel you and watch over you.

Psalm 32:7,8

My soul is weary with sorrow; strengthen me according to your word.

Psalm 119:28

Hatred stirs up dissension, but love covers over all wrongs.

Proverbs 10:12

A friend loves at all times, and a brother is born for adversity.

Proverbs 17:17

So in everything, do to others what you would have them do to you, for this sums up the Law and the Prophets.

Matthew 7:12

A new command I give you: Love one another. As I have loved you, so you must love one another.

John 13:34

I know what it is to be in need, and I know what it is to have plenty. I have learned the secret of being content in any and every situation, whether well fed or hungry, whether living in plenty or in want.

I can do everything through him who gives me strength.

And my God will meet all your needs according to his glorious riches in Christ Jesus.
Philippians 4:12,13,19

Bear with each other and forgive whatever grievances you may have against one another. Forgive as the Lord forgave you.
And over all these virtues put on love, which binds them all together in perfect unity.
Colossians 3:13,14

If any of you lacks wisdom, he should ask God, who gives generously to all without finding fault, and it will be given to him.
James 1:5

But if you harbor bitter envy and selfish ambition in your hearts, do not boast about it or deny the truth.

For where you have envy and selfish ambition, there you find disorder and every evil practice.

But the wisdom that comes from heaven is first of all pure; then peace-loving, considerate, submissive, full of mercy and good fruit, impartial and sincere.

Peacemakers who sow in peace raise a harvest of righteousness.

James 3:14,16-18

Therefore confess your sins to each other and pray for each other so that you may be healed. The prayer of a righteous man is powerful and effective.

James 5:16

When Your Wife Disagrees With You About the Children's Discipline

If you do what is right, will you not be accepted? But if you do not do what is right, sin is crouching at your door; it desires to have you, but you must master it.

Genesis 4:7

These commandments that I give you today are to be upon your hearts.

Impress them on your children. Talk about them when you sit at home and when you walk along the road, when you lie down and when you get up.

Tie them as symbols on your hands and bind them on your foreheads.

Write them on the doorframes of your houses and on your gates.

Deuteronomy 6:6-9

Do not let this Book of the Law depart from your mouth; meditate on it day and night, so that you may be careful to do everything written in it. Then you will be prosperous and successful.

Joshua 1:8

Sons are a heritage from the LORD, children a reward from him.

Psalm 127:3

Children's children are a crown to the aged, and parents are the pride of their children.

Proverbs 17:6

Train a child in the way he should go, and when he is old he will not turn from it.

Proverbs 22:6

The LORD will guide you always; he will satisfy your needs in a sun-scorched land and will strengthen your frame. You will be like a well-watered garden, like a spring whose waters never fail.

Isaiah 58:11

He will turn the hearts of the fathers to their children, and the hearts of the children to their fathers; or else I will come and strike the land with a curse.

Malachi 4:6

Get rid of all bitterness, rage and anger, brawling and slander, along with every form of malice.

Be kind and compassionate to one another, forgiving each other, just as in Christ God forgave you.

Ephesians 4:31,32

But you, man of God, flee from all this, and pursue righteousness, godliness, faith, love, endurance and gentleness.

1 Timothy 6:11

When Your Wife Seems Overly Critical or Abusive

Though an army besiege me, my heart will not fear; though war break out against me, even then will I be confident.

Wait for the LORD; be strong and take heart and wait for the LORD.

Psalm 27:3,14

Since you are my rock and my fortress, for the sake of your name lead and guide me.

Psalm 31:3

You are my hiding place; you will protect me from trouble and surround me with songs of deliverance. Selah.

I will instruct you and teach you in the way you should go; I will counsel you and watch over you.

Psalm 32:7,8

A gentle answer turns away wrath, but a harsh word stirs up anger.

A mocker resents correction; he will not consult the wise.

Proverbs 15:1,12

Blessed are you when people insult you, persecute you and falsely say all kinds of evil against you because of me.

Rejoice and be glad, because great is your reward in heaven, for in the same way they persecuted the prophets who were before you.

Matthew 5:11,12

But I tell you: Love your enemies and pray for those who persecute you, that you may be sons of your Father in heaven. He causes his sun to rise on the evil and the good, and sends rain on the righteous and the unrighteous.

Be perfect, therefore, as your heavenly Father is perfect.

Matthew 5:44,45,48

But I tell you that men will have to give account on the day of judgment for every careless word they have spoken.

For by your words you will be acquitted, and by your words you will be condemned.
Matthew 12:36,37

If your brother sins against you, go and show him his fault, just between the two of you. If he listens to you, you have won your brother over.
Matthew 18:15

Do not let any unwholesome talk come out of your mouths, but only what is helpful for building others up according to their needs, that it may benefit those who listen.

And do not grieve the Holy Spirit of God, with whom you were sealed for the day of redemption.

Get rid of all bitterness, rage and anger, brawling and slander, along with every form of malice.

Be kind and compassionate to one another, forgiving each other, just as in Christ God forgave you.
Ephesians 4:29-32

For we know him who said, "It is mine to avenge; I will repay," and again, "The Lord will judge his people."

Hebrews 10:30

Bear with each other and forgive whatever grievances you may have against one another. Forgive as the Lord forgave you.

And over all these virtues put on love, which binds them all together in perfect unity.

Colossians 3:13,14

But if you harbor bitter envy and selfish ambition in your hearts, do not boast about it or deny the truth.

For where you have envy and selfish ambition, there you find disorder and every evil practice.

But the wisdom that comes from heaven is first of all pure; then peace-loving, considerate, submissive, full of mercy and good fruit, impartial and sincere.

Peacemakers who sow in peace raise a harvest of righteousness.

James 3:14,16-18

Do not repay evil with evil or insult with insult, but with blessing, because to this you were called so that you may inherit a blessing.

For, ''Whoever would love life and see good days must keep his tongue from evil and his lips from deceitful speech.

For the eyes of the Lord are on the righteous and his ears are attentive to their prayer, but the face of the Lord is against those who do evil.''

Keeping a clear conscience, so that those who speak maliciously against your good behavior in Christ may be ashamed of their slander.

It is better, if it is God's will, to suffer for doing good than for doing evil.

1 Peter 3:9,10,12,16,17

When Your Wife Seems Jealous or Overprotective

Keep your tongue from evil and your lips from speaking lies.

Psalm 34:13

Do not fret because of evil men or be envious of those who do wrong.

Psalm 37:1

Do not envy a violent man or choose any of his ways.

Proverbs 3:31

A heart at peace gives life to the body, but envy rots the bones.

Proverbs 14:30

The tongue has the power of life and death, and those who love it will eat its fruit.

Proverbs 18:21

Do not envy wicked men, do not desire their company.

Proverbs 24:1

Place me like a seal over your heart, like a seal on your arm; for love is as strong as death, its jealousy unyielding as the grave. It burns like blazing fire, like a mighty flame.

Song of Solomon 8:6

Do not judge, or you too will be judged.

Matthew 7:1

Let us behave decently, as in the daytime, not in orgies and drunkenness, not in sexual immorality and debauchery, not in dissension and jealousy.

Romans 13:13

You are still worldly. For since there is jealousy and quarreling among you, are you not worldly? Are you not acting like mere men?

1 Corinthians 3:3

Those who belong to Christ Jesus have crucified the sinful nature with its passions and desires.

Since we live by the Spirit, let us keep in step with the Spirit.

Let us not become conceited, provoking and envying each other.

Galatians 5:24-26

Do not let any unwholesome talk come out of your mouths, but only what is helpful for building others up according to their needs, that it may benefit those who listen.

Get rid of all bitterness, rage and anger, brawling and slander, along with every form of malice.

Ephesians 4:29,31

Therefore, rid yourselves of all malice and all deceit, hypocrisy, envy, and slander of every kind.

Like newborn babies, crave pure spiritual milk, so that by it you may grow up in your salvation.

1 Peter 2:1,2

Do not repay evil with evil or insult with insult, but with blessing, because to this you were called so that you may inherit a blessing.

For, "Whoever would love life and see good days must keep his tongue from evil and his lips from deceitful speech."

1 Peter 3:9,10

I will praise the LORD, who counsels me; even at night my heart instructs me.

Jude 1:20

When Your Wife Has Responsibilities Away From Home

But you, dear friends, build yourselves up in your most holy faith and pray in the Holy Spirit.

Psalm 16:7

As for God, his way is perfect; the word of the LORD is flawless. He is a shield for all who take refuge in him.

Psalm 18:30

Teach me your way, O LORD; lead me in a straight path because of my oppressors.

Psalm 27:11

Great peace have they who love your law, and nothing can make them stumble.

Psalm 119:165

The LORD will fulfill for me; your love, O LORD, endures forever — do not abandon the works of your hands.

Psalm 138:8

Trust in the LORD with all your heart and lean not on your own understanding; in all your ways acknowledge him, and he will make your paths straight.

Proverbs 3:5,6

Counsel and sound judgment are mine; I have understanding and power.

Proverbs 8:14

Understanding is a fountain of life to those who have it, but folly brings punishment to fools.

A wise man's heart guides his mouth, and his lips promote instruction.

Proverbs 16:22,23

By wisdom a house is built, and through understanding it is established; through knowledge its rooms are filled with rare and beautiful treasures.

Proverbs 24:3,4

Surely God is my salvation; I will trust and not be afraid. The LORD, the LORD, is my strength and my song; he has become my salvation.

Isaiah 12:2

"For my thoughts are not your thoughts, neither are your ways my ways," declares the LORD.

"As the heavens are higher than the earth, so are my ways higher than your ways and my thoughts than your thoughts."

Isaiah 55:8,9

Call to me and I will answer you and tell you great and unsearchable things you do not know.

Jeremiah 33:3

Do two walk together unless they have agreed to do so?

Amos 3:3

So I say to you: Ask and it will be given to you; seek and you will find; knock and the door will be opened to you.

Luke 11:9

Then he opened their minds so they could understand the Scriptures.

Luke 24:45

Bear with each other and forgive whatever grievances you may have against one another. Forgive as the Lord forgave you.

Colossians 3:13

Your Work

When You Have Become
a Workaholic

Blessed is the man who does not walk in the counsel of the wicked or stand in the way of sinners or sit in the seat of mockers.

But his delight is in the law of the LORD, and on his law he meditates day and night.

He is like a tree planted by streams of water, which yields its fruit in season and whose leaf does not wither. Whatever he does prospers.

Psalm 1:1-3

I will praise the LORD, who counsels me; even at night my heart instructs me.

Psalm 16:7

Show me your ways, O LORD, teach me your paths.

Psalm 25:4

One thing I ask of the LORD, this is what I seek: that I may dwell in the house of the LORD all the days of my life, to gaze upon the beauty of the LORD and to seek him in his temple.

For in the day of trouble he will keep me safe in his dwelling; he will hide me in the shelter of his tabernacle and set me high upon a rock.

Psalm 27:4,5

I will instruct you and teach you in the way you should go; I will counsel you and watch over you.

Psalm 32:8

God is our refuge and strength, an ever-present help in trouble.

Psalm 46:1

Surely you desire truth in the inner parts; you teach me wisdom in the inmost place.

Psalm 51:6

I will say of the LORD, "He is my refuge and my fortress, my God, in whom I trust."

Psalm 91:2

Even in darkness light dawns for the upright, for the gracious and compassionate and righteous man.

Psalm 112:4

The LORD is with me; I will not be afraid. What can man do to me?

It is better to take refuge in the LORD than to trust in man.

Psalm 118:6,8

For the LORD gives wisdom, and from his mouth come knowledge and understanding.

Proverbs 2:6

Trust in the LORD with all your heart and lean not on your own understanding; in all your ways acknowledge him, and he will make your paths straight.

Proverbs 3:5,6

Plans fail for lack of counsel, but with many advisers they succeed.

Proverbs 15:22

Whether you turn to the right or to the left, your ears will hear a voice behind you, saying, "This is the way; walk in it."

Isaiah 30:21

I will lead the blind by ways they have not known, along unfamiliar paths I will guide them; I will turn the darkness into light before them and make the rough places smooth. These are the things I will do; I will not forsake them.

Isaiah 42:16

This is what the LORD says — your Redeemer, the Holy One of Israel: "I am the LORD your God, who teaches you what is best for you, who directs you in the way you should go."

Isaiah 48:17

But when he, the Spirit of truth, comes, he will guide you into all truth. He will not speak on his own; he will speak only what he hears, and he will tell you what is yet to come.

He will bring glory to me by taking from what is mine and making it known to you.

John 16:13,14

What, then, shall we say in response to this? If God is for us, who can be against us?
Romans 8:31

If any of you lacks wisdom, he should ask God, who gives generously to all without finding fault, and it will be given to him.
James 1:5

When You Feel Unusual Stress

The LORD is a refuge for the oppressed, a stronghold in times of trouble.
Psalm 9:9

I love you, O LORD, my strength.

The LORD is my rock, my fortress and my deliverer; my God is my rock, in whom I take refuge. He is my shield and the horn of my salvation, my stronghold.
Psalm 18:1,2

My flesh and my heart may fail, but God is the strength of my heart and my portion forever.
Psalm 73:26

The LORD will indeed give what is good, and our land will yield its harvest.
Psalm 85:12

A thousand may fall at your side, ten thousand at your right hand, but it will not come near you.

If you make the most High your dwelling — even the LORD, who is my refuge — then no harm will befall you, no disaster will come near your tent.

Psalm 91:7,9,10

Praise the LORD, O my soul, and forget not all his benefits — who satisfies your desires with good things so that your youth is renewed like the eagle's.

Psalm 103:2,5

He sent forth his word and healed them; he rescued them from the grave.

Psalm 107:20

May there be peace within your walls and security within your citadels.

Psalm 122:7

In vain you rise early and stay up late, toiling for food to eat — for he grants sleep to those he loves.

Psalm 127:2

When you lie down, you will not be afraid; when you lie down, your sleep will be sweet.
Proverbs 3:24

Wicked men are overthrown and are no more, but the house of the righteous stands firm.
Proverbs 12:7

I tell you the truth, whatever you bind on earth will be bound in heaven, and whatever you loose on earth will be loosed in heaven.
Matthew 18:18

Do not let your hearts be troubled. Trust in God; trust also in me.

Peace I leave with you; my peace I give you. I do not give to you as the world gives. Do not let your hearts be troubled and do not be afraid.
John 14:1,27

Do not be anxious about anything, but in everything, by prayer and petition, with thanksgiving, present your requests to God.

And the peace of God, which transcends all understanding, will guard your hearts and your minds in Christ Jesus.

Philippians 4:6,7

Cast all your anxiety on him because he cares for you.

1 Peter 5:7

When Your Efforts Seem Unappreciated by Others

Be strong and courageous. Do not be afraid or terrified because of them, for the LORD your God goes with you; he will never leave you nor forsake you.

Deuteronomy 31:6

Those who know your name will trust in you, for you, LORD, have never forsaken those who seek you.

Psalm 9:10

As for God, his way is perfect; the word of the LORD is flawless. He is a shield for all who take refuge in him.

Psalm 18:30

May the LORD answer you when you are in distress; may the name of the God of Jacob protect you.

May he send you help from the sanctuary and grant you support from Zion.

Psalm 20:1,2

A righteous man may have many troubles, but the LORD delivers him from them all.

Psalm 34:19

Why are you downcast, O my soul? Why so disturbed within me? Put your hope in God, for I will yet praise him, my Savior and my God.

Psalm 43:5

Find rest, O my soul, in God alone; my hope comes from him.

Psalm 62:5

"Because he loves me," says the LORD, "I will rescue him; I will protect him, for he acknowledges my name.

He will call upon me, and I will answer him; I will be with him in trouble, I will deliver him and honor him.

Psalm 91:14,15

I wait for the LORD, my soul waits, and in his word I put my hope.

Psalm 130:5

Then you will win favor and a good name in the sight of God and man.

Trust in the LORD with all your heart and lean not on your own understanding; in all your ways acknowledge him, and he will make your paths straight.

Proverbs 3:4-6

Above all else, guard your heart, for it is the wellspring of life.

Proverbs 4:23

So do not fear, for I am with you; do not be dismayed, for I am your God. I will strengthen you and help you; I will uphold you with my righteous right hand.

Isaiah 41:10

See, I have engraved you on the palms of my hands; your walls are ever before me.

Isaiah 49:16

Ask and it will be given to you; seek and you will find; knock and the door will be opened to you.

For everyone who asks receives; he who seeks finds; and to him who knocks, the door will be opened.

Matthew 7:7,8

And surely I am with you always, to the very end of the age.

Matthew 28:20b

I have given you authority to trample on snakes and scorpions and to overcome all the power of the enemy; nothing will harm you.

Luke 10:19

And we know that in all things God works for the good of those who love him, who have been called according to his purpose.

For I am convinced that neither death nor life, neither angels nor demons, neither the present nor the future, nor any powers, neither height nor depth, nor anything else in all creation, will be able to separate us from the love of God that is in Christ Jesus our Lord.

Romans 8:28,38,39

What, then, shall we say in response to this? If God is for us, who can be against us?

Romans 8:31

So we say with confidence, ''The Lord is my helper; I will not be afraid. What can man do to me?''

Hebrews 13:6

Cast all your anxiety on him because he cares for you.

1 Peter 5:7

When You Feel Like a Failure

But he knows the way that I take; when he has tested me, I will come forth as gold.

Job 23:10

He will guard the feet of his saints, but the wicked will be silenced in darkness. It is not by strength that one prevails.

1 Samuel 2:9

I will lie down and sleep in peace, for you alone, O LORD, make me dwell in safety.

Psalm 4:8

He who dwells in the shelter of the Most High will rest in the shadow of the Almighty.

I will say of the LORD, "He is my refuge and my fortress, my God, in whom I trust."
Psalm 91:1,2

As far as the east is from the west, so far has he removed our transgressions from us.
Psalm 103:12

When you lie down, you will not be afraid; when you lie down, your sleep will be sweet.
Proverbs 3:24

You will keep in perfect peace him whose mind is steadfast, because he trusts in you.
Isaiah 26:3

I, even I, am he who blots out your transgressions, for my own sake, and remembers your sins no more.
Isaiah 43:25

Let the wicked forsake his way and the evil man his thoughts. Let him turn to the LORD, and he will have mercy on him, and to our God, for he will freely pardon.

Isaiah 55:7

The LORD your God is with you, he is mighty to save. He will take great delight in you, he will quiet you with his love, he will rejoice over you with singing.

Zephaniah 3:17

God made him who had no sin to be sin for us, so that in him we might become the righteousness of God.

2 Corinthians 5:21

But the Lord is faithful, and he will strengthen and protect you from the evil one.

2 Thessalonians 3:3

Let the peace of Christ rule in your hearts, since as members of one body you were called to peace. And be thankful.

Colossians 3:15

For I will forgive their wickedness and will remember their sins no more.

Hebrews 8:12

Cast all your anxiety on him because he cares for you.

1 Peter 5:7

If we confess our sins, he is faithful and just and will forgive us our sins and purify us from all unrighteousness.

1 John 1:9

They overcame him by the blood of the Lamb and by the word of their testimony; they did not love their lives so much as to shrink from death.

Revelation 12:11

When Others Have Unrealistic Expectations of You

My times are in your hands; deliver me from my enemies and from those who pursue me.

Psalm 31:15

When a man's ways are pleasing to the LORD, he makes even his enemies live at peace with him.

Proverbs 16:7

In the same way, let your light shine before men, that they may see your good deeds and praise your Father in heaven.

But I tell you: Love your enemies and pray for those who persecute you.

Matthew 5:16,44

I tell you the truth, if anyone says to this mountain, ''Go, throw yourself into the sea,'' and does not doubt in his heart but believes that what he says will happen, it will be done for him.

Mark 11:23

So watch yourselves. If your brother sins, rebuke him, and if he repents, forgive him.

Luke 17:3

Do not be overcome by evil, but overcome evil with good.

Romans 12:21

Get rid of all bitterness, rage and anger, brawling and slander, along with every form of malice.

Be kind and compassionate to one another, forgiving each other, just as in Christ God forgave you.

Ephesians 4:31,32

Let us then approach the throne of grace with confidence, so that we may receive mercy and find grace to help us in our time of need.

Hebrews 4:16

God is not unjust; he will not forget your work and the love you have shown him as you have helped his people and continue to help them.

Hebrews 6:10

For we know him who said, "It is mine to avenge; I will repay," and again, "The Lord will judge his people."

Hebrews 10:30

When Your Job Is Unfulfilling

Be strong and take heart, all you who hope in the LORD.

Psalm 31:24

I will instruct you and teach you in the way you should go; I will counsel you and watch over you.

Psalm 32:8

I wait for you, O LORD; you will answer, O Lord my God.

Psalm 38:15

Why are you downcast, O my soul? Why so disturbed within me? Put your hope in God, for I will yet praise him, my Savior and my God.

Psalm 43:5

But as for me, I will always have hope; I will praise you more and more.

Psalm 71:14

Blessed is he whose help is the God of Jacob, whose hope is in the LORD his God,

Psalm 146:5

Above all else, guard your heart, for it is the wellspring of life.

Proverbs 4:23

Diligent hands will rule, but laziness ends in slave labor.

Proverbs 12:24

Hope deferred makes the heart sick, but a longing fulfilled is a tree of life.
Proverbs 13:12

Do not love sleep or you will grow poor; stay awake and you will have food to spare.
Proverbs 20:13

Do not let your heart envy sinners, but always be zealous for the fear of the LORD.
There is surely a future hope for you, and your hope will not be cut off.
Proverbs 23:17,18

Whatever your hand finds to do, do it with all your might.
Ecclesiastes 9:10a

As long as it is day, we must do the work of him who sent me. Night is coming, when no one can work.
John 9:4

May the God of hope fill you with all joy and peace as you trust in him, so that you may overflow with hope by the power of the Holy Spirit.

Romans 15:13

Therefore, my dear brothers, stand firm. Let nothing move you. Always give yourselves fully to the work of the Lord, because you know that your labor in the Lord is not in vain.

1 Corinthians 15:58

And God is able to make all grace abound to you, so that in all things at all times, having all that you need, you will abound in every good work.

2 Corinthians 9:8

For when I am weak, then I am strong.

2 Corinthians 12:10b

I pray that out of his glorious riches he may strengthen you with power through his Spirit in your inner being.

Ephesians 3:16

And the peace of God, which transcends all understanding, will guard your hearts and your minds in Christ Jesus.

Philippians 4:7

Now faith is being sure of what we hope for and certain of what we do not see.

And without faith it is impossible to please God, because anyone who comes to him must believe that he exists and that he rewards those who earnestly seek him.

Hebrews 11:1,6

Make it your ambition to lead a quiet life, to mind your own business and to work with your hands, just as we told you, so that your daily life may win the respect of outsiders and so that you will not be dependent on anybody.

1 Thessalonians 4:11,12

Therefore, prepare your minds for action; be self-controlled; set your hope fully on the grace to be given you when Jesus Christ is revealed.

But the word of the Lord stands forever. And this is the word that was preached to you.

1 Peter 1:13,25

When You Make
a Major Career Decision

The LORD himself goes before you and will be with you; he will never leave you nor forsake you. Do not be afraid; do not be discouraged.

Deuteronomy 31:8

Have I not commanded you? Be strong and courageous. Do not be terrified; do not be discouraged, for the LORD your God will be with you wherever you go.

Joshua 1:9

But as for you, be strong and do not give up, for your work will be rewarded.

2 Chronicles 15:7

I will praise the LORD, who counsels me; even at night my heart instructs me.

Psalm 16:7

Show me your ways, O LORD, teach me your paths.

Psalm 25:4

I will instruct you and teach you in the way you should go; I will counsel you and watch over you.

Psalm 32:8

A righteous man may have many troubles, but the LORD delivers him from them all.

Psalm 34:19

God is our refuge and strength, an ever-present help in trouble.

Psalm 46:1

Surely you desire truth in the inner parts; you teach me wisdom in the inmost place.

Psalm 51:6

I will say of the LORD, ''He is my refuge and my fortress, my God, in whom I trust.''

Psalm 91:2

The LORD is with me; I will not be afraid. What can man do to me?

It is better to take refuge in the LORD than to trust in man.

Psalm 118:6,8

Your word, O LORD, is eternal; it stands firm in the heavens.

Psalm 119:89

For the LORD gives wisdom, and from his mouth come knowledge and understanding.

Proverbs 2:6

Trust in the LORD with all your heart and lean not on your own understanding; in all your ways acknowledge him, and he will make your paths straight.

Proverbs 3:5,6

My son, pay attention to what I say; listen closely to my words.

Do not let them out of your sight, keep them within your heart; for they are life to those who find them and health to a man's whole body.

Proverbs 4:20-22

For lack of guidance a nation falls, but many advisers make victory sure.

Proverbs 11:14

Plans fail for lack of counsel, but with many advisers they succeed.

Proverbs 15:22

The name of the LORD is a strong tower; the righteous run to it and are safe.

Proverbs 18:10

Whether you turn to the right or to the left, your ears will hear a voice behind you, saying, "This is the way; walk in it."

Isaiah 30:21

So do not fear, for I am with you; do not be dismayed, for I am your God. I will strengthen you and help you; I will uphold you with my righteous right hand.

Isaiah 41:10

I will lead the blind by ways they have not known, along unfamiliar paths I will guide them; I will turn the darkness into light before them and make the rough places smooth. These are the things I will do; I will not forsake them.

Isaiah 42:16

This is what the LORD says — your Redeemer, the Holy One of Israel: ''I am the LORD your God, who teaches you what is best for you, who directs you in the way you should go.''

Isaiah 48:17

But when he, the Spirit of truth, comes, he will guide you into all truth. He will not speak on his own; he will speak only what he hears, and he will tell you what is yet to come.

He will bring glory to me by taking from what is mine and making it known to you.

John 16:13,14

What, then, shall we say in response to this? If God is for us, who can be against us?

Romans 8:31

Being confident of this, that he who began a good work in you will carry it on to completion until the day of Christ Jesus.

And this is my prayer: that your love may abound more and more in knowledge and depth of insight, so that you may be able to discern what is best and may be pure and blameless until the day of Christ.

Philippians 1:6,9,10

If any of you lacks wisdom, he should ask God, who gives generously to all without finding fault, and it will be given to him.

James 1:5

When You Get Fired From Your Job

O LORD my God, I take refuge in you; save and deliver me from all who pursue me.

Psalm 7:1

Those who know your name will trust in you, for you, LORD, have never forsaken those who seek you.

Psalm 9:10

To you, O LORD, I lift up my soul; in you I trust, O my God. Do not let me be put to shame, nor let my enemies triumph over me.

Psalm 25:1,2

Trust in the LORD and do good; dwell in the land and enjoy safe pasture.

Delight yourself in the LORD and he will give you the desires of your heart.

Commit your way to the LORD; trust in him and he will do this:

He will make your righteousness shine like the dawn, the justice of your cause like the noonday sun.

For evil men will be cut off, but those who hope in the LORD will inherit the land.

If the LORD delights in a man's way, he makes his steps firm; I was young and now I am old, yet I have never seen the righteous forsaken or their children begging bread.

For the LORD loves the just and will not forsake his faithful ones. They will be protected forever, but the offspring of the wicked will be cut off.

Psalm 37:3-6,9,23,25,28

Why are you downcast, O my soul? Why so disturbed within me? Put your hope in God, for I will yet praise him, my Savior and my God.

Psalm 42:5,6a

And call upon me in the day of trouble; I will deliver you, and you will honor me.

Psalm 50:15

"Because he loves me," says the LORD, "I will rescue him; I will protect him, for he acknowledges my name.

He will call upon me, and I will answer him; I will be with him in trouble, I will deliver him and honor him."

Psalm 91:14,15

For the LORD will not reject his people; he will never forsake his inheritance.

Psalm 94:14

Though I walk in the midst of trouble, you preserve my life; you stretch out your hand against the anger of my foes, with your right hand you save me.

The LORD will fulfill for me; your love, O LORD, endures forever — do not abandon the works of your hands.

Psalm 138:7,8

Do not say, "I'll pay you back for this wrong!" Wait for the LORD, and he will deliver you.

Proverbs 20:22

For if you forgive men when they sin against you, your heavenly Father will also forgive you.

Matthew 6:14

If he sins against you seven times in a day, and seven times comes back to you and says, "I repent," forgive him.

Luke 17:4

Do not repay anyone evil for evil. Be careful to do what is right in the eyes of everybody.

Romans 12:17

Love is patient, love is kind. It does not envy, it does not boast, it is not proud.

1 Corinthians 13:4

For our struggle is not against flesh and blood, but against the rulers, against the authorities, against the powers of this dark world and against the spiritual forces of evil in the heavenly realms.

Therefore put on the full armor of God, so that when the day of evil comes, you may be able to stand your ground, and after you have done everything, to stand.

Stand firm then, with the belt of truth buckled around your waist, with the breastplate of righteousness in place, and with your feet fitted with the readiness that comes from the gospel of peace.

In addition to all this, take up the shield of faith, with which you can extinguish all the flaming arrows of the evil one.

Ephesians 6:12-16

And the Lord's servant must not quarrel; instead, he must be kind to everyone, able to teach, not resentful.

2 Timothy 2:24

But the Lord stood at my side and gave me strength, so that through me the message might be fully proclaimed and all the Gentiles might hear it. And I was delivered from the lion's mouth.

The Lord will rescue me from every evil attack and will bring me safely to his heavenly kingdom. To him be glory for ever and ever. Amen.

2 Timothy 4:17,18

Let us then approach the throne of grace with confidence, so that we may receive mercy and find grace to help us in our time of need.

Hebrews 4:16

Dear friends, do not be surprised at the painful trial you are suffering, as though something strange were happening to you.

But rejoice that you participate in the sufferings of Christ, so that you may be overjoyed when his glory is revealed.

1 Peter 4:12,13

Your Daily Schedule

When You Have Over-Booked
Your Schedule

The LORD is a refuge for the oppressed,
a stronghold in times of trouble.

Psalm 9:9

Praise the LORD, O my soul, and forget
not all his benefits — who satisfies your desires
with good things so that your youth is renewed
like the eagle's.

Psalm 103:2,5

Great peace have they who love your law,
and nothing can make them stumble.

Psalm 119:165

For your name's sake, O LORD, preserve
my life; in your righteousness, bring me out
of trouble.

Psalm 143:11

When you lie down, you will not be afraid; when you lie down, your sleep will be sweet.

Proverbs 3:24

Instruct a wise man and he will be wiser still; teach a righteous man and he will add to his learning.

Proverbs 9:9

Wicked men are overthrown and are no more, but the house of the righteous stands firm.

Proverbs 12:7

Better is open rebuke than hidden love.

Proverbs 27:5

But those who hope in the LORD will renew their strength. They will soar on wings like eagles; they will run and not grow weary, they will walk and not be faint.

Isaiah 40:31

Because the Sovereign LORD helps me, I will not be disgraced.

Isaiah 50:7a

I pray that out of his glorious riches he may strengthen you with power through his Spirit in your inner being.

Ephesians 3:16

Finally, be strong in the Lord and in his mighty power.

Ephesians 6:10

Do not be anxious about anything, but in everything, by prayer and petition, with thanksgiving, present your requests to God.

And the peace of God, which transcends all understanding, will guard your hearts and your minds in Christ Jesus.

I can do everything through him who gives me strength.

Philippians 4:6,7,13

If any of you lacks wisdom, he should ask God, who gives generously to all without finding fault, and it will be given to him.

James 1:5

When You Feel Disorganized

The LORD is my shepherd, I shall not be in want.

Psalm 23:1

Show me your ways, O LORD, teach me your paths.

Psalm 25:4

I will instruct you and teach you in the way you should go; I will counsel you and watch over you.

Psalm 32:8

Cast your cares on the LORD and he will sustain you; he will never let the righteous fall.

Psalm 55:22

Trust in the LORD with all your heart and lean not on your own understanding; in all your ways acknowledge him, and he will make your paths straight.

For the LORD will be your confidence and will keep your foot from being snared.
Proverbs 3:5,6,26

I know, O LORD, that a man's life is not his own; it is not for man to direct his steps.
Jeremiah 10:23

Then, because so many people were coming and going that they did not even have a chance to eat, he said to them, "Come with me by yourselves to a quiet place and get some rest."

Mark 6:31

For God is not a God of disorder but of peace. As in all the congregations of the saints.
1 Corinthians 14:33

Therefore, my dear brothers, stand firm. Let nothing move you. Always give yourselves fully to the work of the Lord, because you know that your labor in the Lord is not in vain.
1 Corinthians 15:58

Let us not become weary in doing good, for at the proper time we will reap a harvest if we do not give up.

Galatians 6:9

Do not be anxious about anything, but in everything, by prayer and petition, with thanksgiving, present your requests to God.

And the peace of God, which transcends all understanding, will guard your hearts and your minds in Christ Jesus.

Philippians 4:6,7

For God did not give us a spirit of timidity, but a spirit of power, of love and of self-discipline.

2 Timothy 1:7

If any of you lacks wisdom, he should ask God, who gives generously to all without finding fault, and it will be given to him.

James 1:5

When You Become Frustrated by Unnecessary Interruptions

Trust in the LORD with all your heart and lean not on your own understanding.

Proverbs 3:5

Commit to the LORD whatever you do, and your plans will succeed.

Proverbs 16:3

Fear of man will prove to be a snare, but whoever trusts in the LORD is kept safe.

Proverbs 29:25

But blessed is the man who trusts in the LORD, whose confidence is in him.

He will be like a tree planted by the water that sends out its roots by the stream. It does not fear when heat comes; its leaves are always green. It has no worries in a year of drought and never fails to bear fruit.

Jeremiah 17:7,8

Take my yoke upon you and learn from me, for I am gentle and humble in heart, and you will find rest for your souls.

Matthew 11:29

"If you can?" said Jesus. "Everything is possible for him who believes."

Mark 9:23

So I say to you: Ask and it will be given to you; seek and you will find; knock and the door will be opened to you.

Luke 11:9

If that is how God clothes the grass of the field, which is here today, and tomorrow is thrown into the fire, how much more will he clothe you, O you of little faith!

Luke 12:28

Let us then approach the throne of grace with confidence, so that we may receive mercy and find grace to help us in our time of need.

Hebrews 4:16

We do not want you to become lazy, but to imitate those who through faith and patience inherit what has been promised.

Hebrews 6:12

So do not throw away your confidence; it will be richly rewarded.

But my righteous one will live by faith. And if he shrinks back, I will not be pleased with him.

Hebrews 10:35,38

Keep your lives free from the love of money and be content with what you have, because God has said, "Never will I leave you; never will I forsake you."

Hebrews 13:5

Cast all your anxiety on him because he cares for you.

1 Peter 5:7

When Work Robs You of Important Family Time

By wisdom a house is built, and through understanding it is established.

Proverbs 24:3

But seek first his kingdom and his righteousness, and all these things will be given to you as well.

Matthew 6:33

They replied, ''Believe in the Lord Jesus, and you will be saved — you and your household.''

Acts 16:31

Be joyful in hope, patient in affliction, faithful in prayer.

Romans 12:12

May the God of hope fill you with all joy and peace as you trust in him, so that you may overflow with hope by the power of the Holy Spirit.

Romans 15:13

Love is patient, love is kind. It does not envy, it does not boast, it is not proud.

It is not rude, it is not self-seeking, it is not easily angered, it keeps no record of wrongs.

Love does not delight in evil but rejoices with the truth.

It always protects, always trusts, always hopes, always perseveres.

1 Corinthians 13:4-7

Fathers, do not exasperate your children; instead, bring them up in the training and instruction of the Lord.

Ephesians 6:4

He must manage his own family well and see that his children obey him with proper respect.

(If anyone does not know how to manage his own family, how can he take care of God's church?)

1 Timothy 3:4,5

If any of you lacks wisdom, he should ask God, who gives generously to all without finding fault, and it will be given to him.

James 1:5

When You Need Time Away From the Demands of Others

In my distress I called to the LORD; I called out to my God. From his temple he heard my voice; my cry came to his ears.

2 Samuel 22:7

God is our refuge and strength, an ever-present help in trouble.

Therefore we will not fear, though the earth give way and the mountains fall into the heart of the sea.

Psalm 46:1,2

The LORD will fulfill for me; your love, O LORD, endures forever — do not abandon the works of your hands.

Psalm 138:8

He gives strength to the weary and increases the power of the weak.
Isaiah 40:29

Again Jesus said, ''Peace be with you! As the Father has sent me, I am sending you.''
John 20:21

So we fix our eyes not on what is seen, but on what is unseen. For what is seen is temporary, but what is unseen is eternal.
2 Corinthians 4:18

It is for freedom that Christ has set us free. Stand firm, then, and do not let yourselves be burdened again by a yoke of slavery.

So I say, live by the Spirit, and you will not gratify the desires of the sinful nature.
Galatians 5:1,16

Make it your ambition to lead a quiet life, to mind your own business and to work with your hands, just as we told you, so that your

daily life may win the respect of outsiders and so that you will not be dependent on anybody.
1 Thessalonians 4:11,12

Endure hardship with us like a good soldier of Christ Jesus.
2 Timothy 2:3

Make every effort to live in peace with all men and to be holy; without holiness no one will see the Lord.
Hebrews 12:14

Blessed is the man who perseveres under trial, because when he has stood the test, he will receive the crown of life that God has promised to those who love him.
James 1:12

When Daily Family Devotions Seem Difficult

A good man leaves an inheritance for his children's children, but a sinner's wealth is stored up for the righteous.
Proverbs 13:22

The righteous man leads a blameless life; blessed are his children after him.
Proverbs 20:7

Train a child in the way he should go, and when he is old he will not turn from it.

Proverbs 22:6

The father of a righteous man has great joy; he who has a wise son delights in him.

Proverbs 23:24

By wisdom a house is built, and through understanding it is established.

Proverbs 24:3

Discipline your son, and he will give you peace; he will bring delight to your soul.

Proverbs 29:17

All your sons will be taught by the LORD, and great will be your children's peace.

In righteousness you will be established: Tyranny will be far from you; you will have nothing to fear. Terror will be far removed; it will not come near you.

Isaiah 54:13,14

Tell it to your children, and let your children tell it to their children, and their children to the next generation.

Joel 1:3

But seek first his kingdom and his righteousness, and all these things will be given to you as well.

Matthew 6:33

Fathers, do not exasperate your children; instead, bring them up in the training and instruction of the Lord.

Ephesians 6:4

Fathers, do not embitter your children, or they will become discouraged.

Colossians 3:21

He must manage his own family well and see that his children obey him with proper respect.

(If anyone does not know how to manage his own family, how can he take care of God's church?)

1 Timothy 3:4,5

If anyone does not provide for his relatives, and especially for his immediate family, he has denied the faith and is worse than an unbeliever.

1 Timothy 5:8

Your Finances

When Your Job Security Is Threatened

The LORD is good, a refuge in times of trouble. He cares for those who trust in him.

Nahum 1:7

The LORD is my shepherd, I shall not be in want.

Psalm 23:1

I was young and now I am old, yet I have never seen the righteous forsaken or their children begging bread.

Psalm 37:25

Honor the LORD with your wealth, with the firstfruits of all your crops; then your barns will be filled to overflowing, and your vats will brim over with new wine.

Proverbs 3:9,10

Do you see a man skilled in his work? He will serve before kings; he will not serve before obscure men.

Proverbs 22:29

Whatever your hand finds to do, do it with all your might.

Ecclesiastes 9:10a

Therefore, my dear brothers, stand firm. Let nothing move you. Always give yourselves fully to the work of the Lord, because you know that your labor in the Lord is not in vain.

1 Corinthians 15:58

And my God will meet all your needs according to his glorious riches in Christ Jesus.

Philippians 4:19

Dear friend, I pray that you may enjoy good health and that all may go well with you, even as your soul is getting along well.

3 John 1:2

When You Face Bankruptcy

The LORD bless you and keep you.

Numbers 6:24

For the LORD your God is a merciful God; he will not abandon or destroy you or forget the covenant with your forefathers, which he confirmed to them by oath.

Deuteronomy 4:31

Be strong and courageous. Do not be afraid or terrified because of them, for the LORD your God goes with you; he will never leave you nor forsake you.

The LORD himself goes before you and will be with you; he will never leave you nor forsake you. Do not be afraid; do not be discouraged.

Deuteronomy 31:6,8

At least there is hope for a tree: If it is cut down, it will sprout again, and its new shoots will not fail.

Its roots may grow old in the ground and its stump die in the soil, yet at the scent of water it will bud and put forth shoots like a plant.

Job 14:7-9

He raises the poor from the dust and lifts the needy from the ash heap; he seats them with princes and has them inherit a throne of honor. For the foundations of the earth are the LORD's; upon them he has set the world.

1 Samuel 2:8

But the needy will not always be forgotten, nor the hope of the afflicted ever perish.

Psalm 9:18

Wait for the LORD; be strong and take heart and wait for the LORD.

Psalm 27:14

My times are in your hands; deliver me from my enemies and from those who pursue me.

Let your face shine on your servant; save me in your unfailing love.

Psalm 31:15,16

I was young and now I am old, yet I have never seen the righteous forsaken or their children begging bread.

Psalm 37:25

Make vows to the LORD your God and fulfill them; let all the neighboring lands bring gifts to the One to be feared.

Psalm 76:11

Honor the LORD with your wealth, with the firstfruits of all your crops; then your barns will be filled to overflowing, and your vats will brim over with new wine.

Proverbs 3:9,10

The LORD does not let the righteous go hungry but he thwarts the craving of the wicked.

Lazy hands make a man poor, but diligent hands bring wealth.

The blessing of the LORD brings wealth, and he adds no trouble to it.

Proverbs 10:3,4,22

Though the fig tree does not bud and there are no grapes on the vines, though the olive crop fails and the fields produce no food, though there are no sheep in the pen and no cattle in the stalls, yet I will rejoice in the LORD, I will be joyful in God my Savior.

Habakkuk 3:17,18

"Bring the whole tithe into the storehouse, that there may be food in my house. Test me in this," says the LORD Almighty, "and see if I will not throw open the floodgates of heaven and pour out so much blessing that you will not have room enough for it.

I will prevent pests from devouring your crops, and the vines in your fields will not cast their fruit," says the LORD Almighty.

"Then all the nations will call you blessed, for yours will be a delightful land," says the LORD Almighty.

Malachi 3:10-12

And everyone who has left houses or brothers or sisters or father or mother or children or fields for my sake will receive a hundred times as much and will inherit eternal life.

Matthew 19:29

Give, and it will be given to you. A good measure, pressed down, shaken together and running over, will be poured into your lap. For with the measure you use, it will be measured to you.

Luke 6:38

As he looked up, Jesus saw the rich putting their gifts into the temple treasury.

He also saw a poor widow put in two very small copper coins.

"I tell you the truth," he said, "this poor widow has put in more than all the others.

All these people gave their gifts out of their wealth; but she out of her poverty put in all she had to live on."

Luke 21:1-4

I am not saying this because I am in need, for I have learned to be content whatever the circumstances.

I know what it is to be in need, and I know what it is to have plenty. I have learned the secret of being content in any and every situation, whether well fed or hungry, whether living in plenty or in want.

I can do everything through him who gives me strength.

And my God will meet all your needs according to his glorious riches in Christ Jesus.
Philippians 4:11-13,19

Dear friend, I pray that you may enjoy good health and that all may go well with you, even as your soul is getting along well.
3 John 1:2

When You Need Creative Ideas for Financial Freedom

Now go; I will help you speak and will teach you what to say.

Exodus 4:12

Be strong and very courageous. Be careful to obey all the law my servant Moses gave you; do not turn from it to the right or to the left, that you may be successful wherever you go.

Joshua 1:7

But it is the spirit in a man, the breath of the Almighty, that gives him understanding.

Job 32:8

He may speak in their ears and terrify them with warnings.

Job 33:16

I will praise the LORD, who counsels me; even at night my heart instructs me.

Psalm 16:7

I will instruct you and teach you in the way you should go; I will counsel you and watch over you.

Psalm 32:8

For with you is the fountain of life; in your light we see light.

Psalm 36:9

The LORD will fulfill for me; your love, O LORD, endures forever — do not abandon the works of your hands.

Psalm 138:8

Let the wise listen and add to their learning, and let the discerning get guidance.

Proverbs 1:5

Wisdom is supreme; therefore get wisdom. Though it cost all you have, get understanding.

Proverbs 4:7

Esteem her, and she will exalt you; embrace her, and she will honor you.

Proverbs 4:8

I love those who love me, and those who seek me find me.

Proverbs 8:17

With me are riches and honor, enduring wealth and prosperity.

Proverbs 8:18

Bestowing wealth on those who love me and making their treasuries full.

Proverbs 8:21

The plans of the righteous are just, but the advice of the wicked is deceitful.

Proverbs 12:5

He who walks with the wise grows wise, but a companion of fools suffers harm.

Proverbs 18:15

The heart of the discerning acquires knowledge; the ears of the wise seek it out.

Proverbs 13:20

Know also that wisdom is sweet to your soul; if you find it, there is a future hope for you, and your hope will not be cut off.

Proverbs 24:14

See, the former things have taken place, and new things I declare; before they spring into being I announce them to you.

Isaiah 42:9

Forget the former things; do not dwell on the past.

See, I am doing a new thing! Now it springs up; do you not perceive it? I am making a way in the desert and streams in the wasteland.

Isaiah 43:18,19

Who despises the day of small things? Men will rejoice when they see the plumb line in the hand of Zerubbabel. "(These seven are the eyes of the LORD, which range throughout the earth.)"

Zechariah 4:10

Ask and it will be given to you; seek and you will find; knock and the door will be opened to you.

Matthew 7:7

Suppose one of you wants to build a tower. Will he not first sit down and estimate the cost to see if he has enough money to complete it?

Luke 14:28

Because you know that the Lord will reward everyone for whatever good he does, whether he is slave or free.

Ephesians 6:8

Finally, brothers, whatever is true, whatever is noble, whatever is right, whatever is pure, whatever is lovely, whatever is admirable — if anything is excellent or praiseworthy — think about such things.

Philippians 4:8

When You Have Spent Money Unwisely

If my people, who are called by my name, will humble themselves and pray and seek my face and turn from their wicked ways, then will I hear from heaven and will forgive their sin and will heal their land.

2 Chronicles 7:14

Plans fail for lack of counsel, but with many advisers they succeed.

Proverbs 22:29

Do you see a man skilled in his work? He will serve before kings; he will not serve before obscure men.

Proverbs 15:22

I will repay you for the years the locusts have eaten — the great locust and the young locust, the other locusts and the locust swarm — my great army that I sent among you.

You will have plenty to eat, until you are full, and you will praise the name of the LORD your God, who has worked wonders for you; never again will my people be shamed.

Joel 2:25,26

And God is able to make all grace abound to you, so that in all things at all times, having all that you need, you will abound in every good work.

2 Corinthians 9:8

For we do not have a high priest who is unable to sympathize with our weaknesses, but we have one who has been tempted in every way, just as we are — yet was without sin.

Hebrews 4:15

If we confess our sins, he is faithful and just and will forgive us our sins and purify us from all unrighteousness.

1 John 1:9

When You Need Wisdom About Borrowing Money

For the LORD gives wisdom, and from his mouth come knowledge and understanding.

Proverbs 2:6

Trust in the LORD with all your heart and lean not on your own understanding.

Proverbs 3:5

Lazy hands make a man poor, but diligent hands bring wealth.

Proverbs 10:4

Diligent hands will rule, but laziness ends in slave labor.

Proverbs 12:24

The sluggard craves and gets nothing, but the desires of the diligent are fully satisfied.

Proverbs 13:4

Plans fail for lack of counsel, but with many advisers they succeed.

Proverbs 15:22

Do not love sleep or you will grow poor; stay awake and you will have food to spare.

Proverbs 20:13

Do you see a man skilled in his work? He will serve before kings; he will not serve before obscure men.

Proverbs 22:29

By wisdom a house is built, and through understanding it is established.

Proverbs 24:3

He who works his land will have abundant food, but the one who chases fantasies will have his fill of poverty.

Proverbs 28:19

Sow your seed in the morning, and at evening let not your hands be idle, for you do not know which will succeed, whether this or that, or whether both will do equally well.

Ecclesiastes 11:6

So do not fear, for I am with you; do not be dismayed, for I am your God. I will strengthen you and help you; I will uphold you with my righteous right hand.

Isaiah 41:10

But seek first his kingdom and his righteousness, and all these things will be given to you as well.

Matthew 6:33

Never be lacking in zeal, but keep your spiritual fervor, serving the Lord.

Romans 12:11

When Tithing Seems Difficult

And blessed be God Most High, who delivered your enemies into your hand. Then Abram gave him a tenth of everything.

Genesis 14:20

But remember the LORD your God, for it is he who gives you the ability to produce wealth, and so confirms his covenant, which he swore to your forefathers, as it is today.

Deuteronomy 8:18

Be sure to set aside a tenth of all that your fields produce each year.

Deuteronomy 14:22

He who is kind to the poor lends to the LORD, and he will reward him for what he has done.

Proverbs 19:17

He who gives to the poor will lack nothing, but he who closes his eyes to them receives many curses.

Proverbs 28:27

"Bring the whole tithe into the storehouse, that there may be food in my house. Test me in this," says the LORD Almighty, "and see if I will not throw open the floodgates of heaven and pour out so much blessing that you will not have room enough for it.

I will prevent pests from devouring your crops, and the vines in your fields will not cast their fruit," says the LORD Almighty.

Malachi 3:10,11

Give, and it will be given to you. A good measure, pressed down, shaken together and running over, will be poured into your lap. For with the measure you use, it will be measured to you.

Luke 6:38

On the first day of every week, each one of you should set aside a sum of money in keeping with his income, saving it up, so that when I come no collections will have to be made.

1 Corinthians 16:2

Remember this: Whoever sows sparingly will also reap sparingly, and whoever sows generously will also reap generously.

Each man should give what he has decided in his heart to give, not reluctantly or under compulsion, for God loves a cheerful giver.

And God is able to make all grace abound to you, so that in all things at all times, having all that you need, you will abound in every good work.

2 Corinthians 9:6-8

And my God will meet all your needs according to his glorious riches in Christ Jesus.
Philippians 4:19

If anyone has material possessions and sees his brother in need but has no pity on him, how can the love of God be in him?

Dear children, let us not love with words or tongue but with actions and in truth.
1 John 3:17,18

When Your Children Need To Learn the Blessing of Work

But as for you, be strong and do not give up, for your work will be rewarded.
2 Chronicles 15:7

The sluggard craves and gets nothing, but the desires of the diligent are fully satisfied.
Proverbs 13:4

The plans of the diligent lead to profit as surely as haste leads to poverty.

Proverbs 21:5

Do you see a man skilled in his work? He will serve before kings; he will not serve before obscure men.

Proverbs 22:29

As long as it is day, we must do the work of him who sent me. Night is coming, when no one can work.

John 9:4

Now to him who is able to do immeasurably more than all we ask or imagine, according to his power that is at work within us.

Ephesians 3:20

I can do everything through him who gives me strength.

Philippians 4:13

Be wise in the way you act toward outsiders; make the most of every opportunity.

Colossians 4:5

If any of you lacks wisdom, he should ask God, who gives generously to all without finding fault, and it will be given to him.

James 1:5

So then, dear friends, since you are looking forward to this, make every effort to be found spotless, blameless and at peace with him.

2 Peter 3:14

I know your deeds. See, I have placed before you an open door that no one can shut. I know that you have little strength, yet you have kept my word and have not denied my name.

Revelation 3:8

Your Church

When Church Conflicts Disillusion You

In you I trust, O my God. Do not let me be put to shame, nor let my enemies triumph over me.

Psalm 25:2

The LORD is my strength and my shield; my heart trusts in him, and I am helped. My heart leaps for joy and I will give thanks to him in song.

Psalm 28:7

But as for me, I watch in hope for the LORD, I wait for God my Savior; my God will hear me.

Do not gloat over me, my enemy! Though I have fallen, I will rise. Though I sit in darkness, the LORD will be my light.

Micah 7:7,8

Though the fig tree does not bud and there are no grapes on the vines, though the olive crop fails and the fields produce no food, though there are no sheep in the pen and no cattle in the stalls, yet I will rejoice in the LORD, I will be joyful in God my Savior.

The Sovereign LORD is my strength; he makes my feet like the feet of a deer, he enables me to go on the heights. For the director of music. On my stringed instruments.

Habakkuk 3:17-19

Therefore we do not lose heart. Though outwardly we are wasting away, yet inwardly we are being renewed day by day.

2 Corinthians 4:16

We live by faith, not by sight.

2 Corinthians 5:7

That is why I am suffering as I am. Yet I am not ashamed, because I know whom I have believed, and am convinced that he is able to guard what I have entrusted to him for that day.

2 Timothy 1:12

Therefore, strengthen your feeble arms and weak knees.

Make level paths for your feet, so that the lame may not be disabled, but rather healed.

Make every effort to live in peace with all men and to be holy; without holiness no one will see the Lord.

See to it that no one misses the grace of God and that no bitter root grows up to cause trouble and defile many.

Hebrews 12:12-15

When Someone Has Offended You

Do not seek revenge or bear a grudge against one of your people, but love your neighbor as yourself. I am the LORD.

Leviticus 19:18

O LORD my God, I take refuge in you; save and deliver me from all who pursue me.

Psalm 7:1

Those who know your name will trust in you, for you, LORD, have never forsaken those who seek you.

Psalm 9:10

"Because he loves me," says the LORD, "I will rescue him; I will protect him, for he acknowledges my name.

He will call upon me, and I will answer him; I will be with him in trouble, I will deliver him and honor him."

Psalm 91:14,15

For the LORD will not reject his people; he will never forsake his inheritance.

Psalm 94:14

A fool shows his annoyance at once, but a prudent man overlooks an insult.

Proverbs 12:16

Do not say, "I'll pay you back for this wrong!" Wait for the LORD, and he will deliver you.

Proverbs 20:22

But I tell you that anyone who is angry with his brother will be subject to judgment. Again, anyone who says to his brother, "Raca," is answerable to the Sanhedrin. But anyone who says, "You fool!" will be in danger of the fire of hell.

Matthew 5:22

For if you forgive men when they sin against you, your heavenly Father will also forgive you.

Matthew 6:14

If he sins against you seven times in a day, and seven times comes back to you and says, "I repent," forgive him.

Luke 17:4

Do not repay anyone evil for evil. Be careful to do what is right in the eyes of everybody.

Romans 12:17

Love is patient, love is kind. It does not envy, it does not boast, it is not proud.

1 Corinthians 13:4

But now you must rid yourselves of all such things as these: anger, rage, malice, slander, and filthy language from your lips.

Colossians 3:8

And the Lord's servant must not quarrel; instead, he must be kind to everyone, able to teach, not resentful.

2 Timothy 2:24

But the Lord stood at my side and gave me strength, so that through me the message might be fully proclaimed and all the Gentiles might hear it. And I was delivered from the lion's mouth.

The Lord will rescue me from every evil attack and will bring me safely to his heavenly kingdom. To him be glory for ever and ever. Amen.

2 Timothy 4:17,18

When You Are Asked To Accept Special Responsibilities

You are the salt of the earth. But if the salt loses its saltiness, how can it be made salty again? It is no longer good for anything, except to be thrown out and trampled by men.

You are the light of the world. A city on a hill cannot be hidden.

Neither do people light a lamp and put it under a bowl. Instead they put it on its stand, and it gives light to everyone in the house.

In the same way, let your light shine before men, that they may see your good deeds and praise your Father in heaven.

Matthew 5:13-16

And if anyone gives even a cup of cold water to one of these little ones because he is my disciple, I tell you the truth, he will certainly not lose his reward.

Matthew 10:42

Just as the Son of Man did not come to be served, but to serve, and to give his life as a ransom for many.

Matthew 20:28

For I was hungry and you gave me something to eat, I was thirsty and you gave me something to drink, I was a stranger and you invited me in, I needed clothes and you clothed me, I was sick and you looked after me, I was in prison and you came to visit me.

Then the righteous will answer him, ''Lord, when did we see you hungry and feed you, or thirsty and give you something to drink?

When did we see you a stranger and invite you in, or needing clothes and clothe you?

When did we see you sick or in prison and go to visit you?''

The King will reply, ''I tell you the truth, whatever you did for one of the least of these brothers of mine, you did for me.''

Matthew 25:35-40

He said to them, ''Go into all the world and preach the good news to all creation.''

Mark 16:15

But you will receive power when the Holy Spirit comes on you; and you will be my witnesses in Jerusalem, and in all Judea and Samaria, and to the ends of the earth.

Acts 1:8

Do not neglect your gift, which was given you through a prophetic message when the body of elders laid their hands on you.

1 Timothy 4:14

When You Feel Unqualified for a Church Position

Then Caleb silenced the people before Moses and said, "We should go up and take possession of the land, for we can certainly do it."

Numbers 13:30

But you will receive power when the Holy Spirit comes on you; and you will be my witnesses in Jerusalem, and in all Judea and Samaria, and to the ends of the earth.

Acts 1:8

But God chose the foolish things of the world to shame the wise; God chose the weak things of the world to shame the strong.

1 Corinthians 1:27

To one there is given through the Spirit the message of wisdom, to another the message of knowledge by means of the same Spirit.

1 Corinthians 12:8

And God is able to make all grace abound to you, so that in all things at all times, having all that you need, you will abound in every good work.

2 Corinthians 9:8

But he said to me, "My grace is sufficient for you, for my power is made perfect in weakness." Therefore I will boast all the more gladly about my weaknesses, so that Christ's power may rest on me.

2 Corinthians 12:9

Now to him who is able to do immeasurably more than all we ask or imagine, according to his power that is at work within us.

Ephesians 3:20

I can do everything through him who gives me strength.

Philippians 4:13

So do not throw away your confidence; it will be richly rewarded.

You need to persevere so that when you have done the will of God, you will receive what he has promised.

Hebrews 10:35,36

By faith Abraham, even though he was past age — and Sarah herself was barren — was enabled to become a father because he considered him faithful who had made the promise.

Hebrews 11:11

If any of you lacks wisdom, he should ask God, who gives generously to all without finding fault, and it will be given to him.

James 1:5

When You Find It Difficult To Be the Spiritual Leader in Your Home

That you may tell your children and grandchildren how I dealt harshly with the Egyptians and how I performed my signs among them, and that you may know that I am the LORD.

Exodus 10:2

On that day tell your son, "I do this because of what the LORD did for me when I came out of Egypt."

Exodus 13:8

Only be careful, and watch yourselves closely so that you do not forget the things your eyes have seen or let them slip from your heart as long as you live. Teach them to your children and to their children after them.

Deuteronomy 4:9

Counsel and sound judgment are mine; I have understanding and power.

Proverbs 8:14

So do not fear, for I am with you; do not be dismayed, for I am your God. I will strengthen you and help you; I will uphold you with my righteous right hand.

Isaiah 41:10

The Sovereign LORD is my strength; he makes my feet like the feet of a deer, he enables me to go on the heights. For the director of music. On my stringed instruments.

Habakkuk 3:19

But you will receive power when the Holy Spirit comes on you; and you will be my witnesses in Jerusalem, and in all Judea and Samaria, and to the ends of the earth.

Acts 1:8

Now to him who is able to do immeasurably more than all we ask or imagine, according to his power that is at work within us.

Ephesians 3:20

I can do everything through him who gives me strength.

Philippians 4:13

Being strengthened with all power according to his glorious might so that you may have great endurance and patience, and joyfully giving thanks to the Father, who has qualified you to share in the inheritance of the saints in the kingdom of light.

Colossians 1:11,12

So do not throw away your confidence; it will be richly rewarded.

You need to persevere so that when you have done the will of God, you will receive what he has promised.

Hebrews 10:35,36

When a Spiritual Mentor Fails

Keep me as the apple of your eye; hide me in the shadow of your wings.

Psalm 17:8

For in the day of trouble he will keep me safe in his dwelling; he will hide me in the shelter of his tabernacle and set me high upon a rock.

Psalm 27:5

Just as the Son of Man did not come to be served, but to serve, and to give his life as a ransom for many.

Matthew 20:28

Not so with you. Instead, whoever wants to become great among you must be your servant, and whoever wants to be first must be slave of all.

Mark 10:43,44

The expert in the law replied, ''The one who had mercy on him.'' Jesus told him, ''Go and do likewise.''

Luke 10:37

The son said to him, ''Father, I have sinned against heaven and against you. I am no longer worthy to be called your son.''

But the father said to his servants, ''Quick! Bring the best robe and put it on him. Put a ring on his finger and sandals on his feet.

Bring the fattened calf and kill it. Let's have a feast and celebrate.

For this son of mine was dead and is alive again; he was lost and is found." So they began to celebrate.

Luke 15:21-24

May the God who gives endurance and encouragement give you a spirit of unity among yourselves as you follow Christ Jesus, so that with one heart and mouth you may glorify the God and Father of our Lord Jesus Christ.

Accept one another, then, just as Christ accepted you, in order to bring praise to God.

Romans 15:5-7

Now it is required that those who have been given a trust must prove faithful.

1 Corinthians 4:2

Therefore, my dear brothers, stand firm. Let nothing move you. Always give yourselves fully to the work of the Lord, because you know that your labor in the Lord is not in vain.

1 Corinthians 15:58

Brothers, if someone is caught in a sin, you who are spiritual should restore him gently. But watch yourself, or you also may be tempted.

Carry each other's burdens, and in this way you will fulfill the law of Christ.

Therefore, as we have opportunity, let us do good to all people, especially to those who belong to the family of believers.

Galatians 6:1,2,10

Be imitators of God, therefore, as dearly loved children and live a life of love, just as Christ loved us and gave himself up for us as a fragrant offering and sacrifice to God.

Ephesians 5:1,2

Slaves, obey your earthly masters with respect and fear, and with sincerity of heart, just as you would obey Christ.

Serve wholeheartedly, as if you were serving the Lord, not men.

Ephesians 6:5,7

Bear with each other and forgive whatever grievances you may have against one another. Forgive as the Lord forgave you.

Slaves, obey your earthly masters in everything; and do it, not only when their eye is on you and to win their favor, but with sincerity of heart and reverence for the Lord.
Colossians 3:13,22

Let us fix our eyes on Jesus, the author and perfecter of our faith, who for the joy set before him endured the cross, scorning its shame, and sat down at the right hand of the throne of God.

Consider him who endured such opposition from sinful men, so that you will not grow weary and lose heart.
Hebrews 12:2,3

To this you were called, because Christ suffered for you, leaving you an example, that you should follow in his steps.
1 Peter 2:21

If we confess our sins, he is faithful and just and will forgive us our sins and purify us from all unrighteousness.

1 John 1:9

For everything in the world — the cravings of sinful man, the lust of his eyes and the boasting of what he has and does — comes not from the Father but from the world.

1 John 2:16

This is how we know what love is: Jesus Christ laid down his life for us. And we ought to lay down our lives for our brothers.

1 John 3:16

Those whom I love I rebuke and discipline. So be earnest, and repent.

Revelation 3:19

Your Personal Needs

When You Need
Personal Motivation

No man will be able to stand against you.
The LORD your God, as he promised you,
will put the terror and fear of you on the whole
land, wherever you go.

Deuteronomy 11:25

The LORD will grant that the enemies who
rise up against you will be defeated before you.
They will come at you from one direction but
flee from you in seven.

Deuteronomy 28:7

Be strong and courageous. Do not be afraid
or terrified because of them, for the LORD
your God goes with you; he will never leave
you nor forsake you.

Deuteronomy 31:6

Be strong and courageous, because you will lead these people to inherit the land I swore to their forefathers to give them.

Joshua 1:6

The LORD has driven out before you great and powerful nations; to this day no one has been able to withstand you.

Joshua 23:9

But David found strength in the LORD his God.

1 Samuel 30:6b

"Don't be afraid," the prophet answered. "Those who are with us are more than those who are with them."

2 Kings 6:16

The Spirit of the Sovereign LORD is on me, because the LORD has anointed me to preach good news to the poor. He has sent me to bind up the brokenhearted, to proclaim freedom for the captives and release from darkness for the prisoners.

Isaiah 61:1

Those who are wise will shine like the brightness of the heavens, and those who lead

many to righteousness, like the stars for ever
and ever.

Daniel 12:3

Ask and it will be given to you; seek and
you will find; knock and the door will be
opened to you.

For everyone who asks receives; he who
seeks finds; and to him who knocks, the door
will be opened.

Matthew 7:7,8

And I tell you that you are Peter, and on
this rock I will build my church, and the gates
of Hades will not overcome it.

I will give you the keys of the kingdom of
heaven; whatever you bind on earth will be
bound in heaven, and whatever you loose on
earth will be loosed in heaven.

Matthew 16:18,19

Then you will know the truth, and the truth
will set you free.

So if the Son sets you free, you will be free
indeed.

John 8:32,36

I tell you the truth, anyone who has faith in me will do what I have been doing. He will do even greater things than these, because I am going to the Father.

John 14:12

But you will receive power when the Holy Spirit comes on you; and you will be my witnesses in Jerusalem, and in all Judea and Samaria, and to the ends of the earth.

Acts 1:8

The weapons we fight with are not the weapons of the world. On the contrary, they have divine power to demolish strongholds.

2 Corinthians 10:4

For it is light that makes everything visible. This is why it is said: ''Wake up, O sleeper, rise from the dead, and Christ will shine on you.''

Ephesians 5:14

I can do everything through him who gives me strength.

Philippians 4:13

Being strengthened with all power according to his glorious might so that you may have great endurance and patience, and joyfully giving thanks to the Father, who has qualified you to share in the inheritance of the saints in the kingdom of light.

Colossians 1:11,12

Be wise in the way you act toward outsiders; make the most of every opportunity.

Colossians 4:5

Be diligent in these matters; give yourself wholly to them, so that everyone may see your progress.

1 Timothy 4:15

You, dear children, are from God and have overcome them, because the one who is in you is greater than the one who is in the world.

In this way, love is made complete among us so that we will have confidence on the day of judgment, because in this world we are like him.

1 John 4:4,17

Dear friend, I pray that you may enjoy good health and that all may go well with you, even as your soul is getting along well.

3 John 1:2

When You Need Inner Peace

I will lie down and sleep in peace, for you alone, O LORD, make me dwell in safety.

Psalm 4:8

Who, then, is the man that fears the LORD? He will instruct him in the way chosen for him.

He will spend his days in prosperity, and his descendants will inherit the land.

Psalm 25:12,13

You will keep in perfect peace him whose mind is steadfast, because he trusts in you.

LORD, you establish peace for us; all that we have accomplished you have done for us.

Isaiah 26:3,12

You will go out in joy and be led forth in peace; the mountains and hills will burst into song before you, and all the trees of the field will clap their hands.

Isaiah 55:12

Those who walk uprightly enter into peace; they find rest as they lie in death.

Isaiah 57:2

Peace I leave with you; my peace I give you. I do not give to you as the world gives. Do not let your hearts be troubled and do not be afraid.

John 14:27

I have told you these things, so that in me you may have peace. In this world you will have trouble. But take heart! I have overcome the world.

John 16:33

Therefore, since we have been justified through faith, we have peace with God through our Lord Jesus Christ.

Romans 5:1

The mind of sinful man is death, but the mind controlled by the Spirit is life and peace.

Romans 8:6

May the God of hope fill you with all joy and peace as you trust in him, so that you may overflow with hope by the power of the Holy Spirit.

Romans 15:13

Finally, brothers, good-by. Aim for perfection, listen to my appeal, be of one mind, live in peace. And the God of love and peace will be with you.

2 Corinthians 13:11

Grace and peace to you from God our Father and the Lord Jesus Christ.

Galatians 1:3

But the fruit of the Spirit is love, joy, peace, patience, kindness, goodness, faithfulness.

Galatians 5:22

For he himself is our peace, who has made the two one and has destroyed the barrier, the dividing wall of hostility.

Ephesians 2:14

Do not be anxious about anything, but in everything, by prayer and petition, with thanksgiving, present your requests to God.

And the peace of God, which transcends all understanding, will guard your hearts and your minds in Christ Jesus.

Whatever you have learned or received or heard from me, or seen in me — put it into practice. And the God of peace will be with you.

Philippians 4:6,7,9

Let the peace of Christ rule in your hearts, since as members of one body you were called to peace. And be thankful.

Colossians 3:15

Now may the Lord of peace himself give you peace at all times and in every way. The Lord be with all of you.

2 Thessalonians 3:16

But the wisdom that comes from heaven is first of all pure; then peace-loving, considerate, submissive, full of mercy and good fruit, impartial and sincere.

Peacemakers who sow in peace raise a harvest of righteousness.

James 3:17,18

When You Need To Forgive

But I tell you: Love your enemies and pray for those who persecute you.

Matthew 5:44

Forgive us our debts, as we also have forgiven our debtors.

And lead us not into temptation, but deliver us from the evil one.

For if you forgive men when they sin against you, your heavenly Father will also forgive you.

But if you do not forgive men their sins, your Father will not forgive your sins.

Matthew 6:12-15

Then Peter came to Jesus and asked, "Lord, how many times shall I forgive my brother when he sins against me? Up to seven times?"

Matthew 18:21

Jesus answered, "I tell you, not seven times, but seventy-seven times."

Matthew 18:22

And when you stand praying, if you hold anything against anyone, forgive him, so that your Father in heaven may forgive you your sins.

Mark 11:25

So watch yourselves. If your brother sins, rebuke him, and if he repents, forgive him.

If he sins against you seven times in a day, and seven times comes back to you and says, "I repent," forgive him.

Luke 17:3,4

If you forgive anyone his sins, they are forgiven; if you do not forgive them, they are not forgiven.

John 20:23

Bless those who persecute you; bless and do not curse.

Do not be overcome by evil, but overcome evil with good.

Romans 12:14,21

Be kind and compassionate to one another, forgiving each other, just as in Christ God forgave you.

Ephesians 4:32

Bear with each other and forgive whatever grievances you may have against one another. Forgive as the Lord forgave you.

Colossians 3:13

Do not repay evil with evil or insult with insult, but with blessing, because to this you were called so that you may inherit a blessing.

1 Peter 3:9

When You Need To Apologize

Then the LORD your God will restore your fortunes and have compassion on you and gather you again from all the nations where he scattered you.

Deuteronomy 30:3

If my people, who are called by my name, will humble themselves and pray and seek my face and turn from their wicked ways, then will I hear from heaven and will forgive their sin and will heal their land.

2 Chronicles 7:14

Cast your cares on the LORD and he will sustain you; he will never let the righteous fall.

Psalm 55:22

The LORD will fulfill for me; your love, O LORD, endures forever — do not abandon the works of your hands.

Psalm 138:8

So do not fear, for I am with you; do not be dismayed, for I am your God. I will strengthen you and help you; I will uphold you with my righteous right hand.

Isaiah 41:10

I will repay you for the years the locusts have eaten — the great locust and the young locust, the other locusts and the locust swarm — my great army that I sent among you.

Joel 2:25

And we know that in all things God works for the good of those who love him, who have been called according to his purpose.

Romans 8:28

We live by faith, not by sight.
>   *2 Corinthians 5:7*

Brothers, if someone is caught in a sin, you who are spiritual should restore him gently. But watch yourself, or you also may be tempted.

Carry each other's burdens, and in this way you will fulfill the law of Christ.
>   *Galatians 6:1,2*

Do nothing out of selfish ambition or vain conceit, but in humility consider others better than yourselves.
>   *Philippians 2:3*

Brothers, I do not consider myself yet to have taken hold of it. But one thing I do: Forgetting what is behind and straining toward what is ahead, I press on toward the goal to win the prize for which God has called me heavenward in Christ Jesus.
>   *Philippians 3:13,14*

Let us hold unswervingly to the hope we profess, for he who promised is faithful.
>   *Hebrews 10:23*

And without faith it is impossible to please God, because anyone who comes to him must believe that he exists and that he rewards those who earnestly seek him.

Hebrews 11:6

These have come so that your faith — of greater worth than gold, which perishes even though refined by fire — may be proved genuine and may result in praise, glory and honor when Jesus Christ is revealed.

1 Peter 1:7

But you are a chosen people, a royal priesthood, a holy nation, a people belonging to God, that you may declare the praises of him who called you out of darkness into his wonderful light.

1 Peter 2:9

Cast all your anxiety on him because he cares for you.

1 Peter 5:7

When You Need Physical Healing

My son, pay attention to what I say; listen closely to my words.

Do not let them out of your sight, keep them within your heart; for they are life to those who find them and health to a man's whole body.

Proverbs 4:20-22

A cheerful heart is good medicine, but a crushed spirit dries up the bones.

Proverbs 17:22

Surely he took up our infirmities and carried our sorrows, yet we considered him stricken by God, smitten by him, and afflicted.

But he was pierced for our transgressions, he was crushed for our iniquities; the punishment that brought us peace was upon him, and by his wounds we are healed.

Isaiah 53:4,5

"But I will restore you to health and heal your wounds," declares the LORD.

Jeremiah 30:17a

Jesus said to him, "I will go and heal him."

Matthew 8:7

"Who touched me?" Jesus asked. When they all denied it, Peter said, "Master, the people are crowding and pressing against you."

But Jesus said, "Someone touched me; I know that power has gone out from me."

Then the woman, seeing that she could not go unnoticed, came trembling and fell at his feet. In the presence of all the people, she told why she had touched him and how she had been instantly healed.

Luke 8:45-47

Jesus Christ is the same yesterday and today and forever.

Hebrews 13:8

Is any one of you in trouble? He should pray. Is anyone happy? Let him sing songs of praise.

Is any one of you sick? He should call the elders of the church to pray over him and anoint him with oil in the name of the Lord.

And the prayer offered in faith will make the sick person well; the Lord will raise him up. If he has sinned, he will be forgiven.

Therefore confess your sins to each other and pray for each other so that you may be healed. The prayer of a righteous man is powerful and effective.

James 5:13-16

Dear friend, I pray that you may enjoy good health and that all may go well with you, cven as your soul is getting along well.

3 John 1:2

When You Need Wisdom

That night God appeared to Solomon and said to him, ''Ask for whatever you want me to give you.''

Solomon answered God, ''You have shown great kindness to David my father and have made me king in his place.

Now, LORD God, let your promise to my father David be confirmed, for you have made me king over a people who are as numerous as the dust of the earth.

Give me wisdom and knowledge, that I may lead this people, for who is able to govern this great people of yours?''

God said to Solomon, ''Since this is your heart's desire and you have not asked for wealth, riches or honor, nor for the death of your enemies, and since you have not asked for a long life but for wisdom and knowledge to govern my people over whom I have made you king, therefore wisdom and knowledge will be given you. And I will also give you wealth, riches and honor, such as no king who was before you ever had and none after you will have.''

2 Chronicles 1:7-12

For the LORD gives wisdom, and from his mouth come knowledge and understanding.

He holds victory in store for the upright, he is a shield to those whose walk is blameless.

Proverbs 2:6,7

Trust in the LORD with all your heart and lean not on your own understanding; in all your ways acknowledge him, and he will make your paths straight.

Proverbs 3:5,6

Wisdom is supreme; therefore get wisdom. Though it cost all you have, get understanding.

Esteem her, and she will exalt you; embrace her, and she will honor you.

Proverbs 4:7,8

Whoever loves discipline loves knowledge, but he who hates correction is stupid.

Proverbs 12:1

Whoever gives heed to instruction prospers, and blessed is he who trusts in the LORD.

The wise in heart are called discerning, and pleasant words promote instruction.

Understanding is a fountain of life to those who have it, but folly brings punishment to fools.

A wise man's heart guides his mouth, and his lips promote instruction.

Proverbs 16:20-23

By wisdom a house is built, and through understanding it is established; through knowledge its rooms are filled with rare and beautiful treasures.

Proverbs 24:3,4

Be wise, my son, and bring joy to my heart; then I can answer anyone who treats me with contempt.

Proverbs 27:11

For I will give you words and wisdom that none of your adversaries will be able to resist or contradict.

Luke 21:15

But when he, the Spirit of truth, comes, he will guide you into all truth. He will not speak on his own; he will speak only what he hears, and he will tell you what is yet to come.

He will bring glory to me by taking from what is mine and making it known to you.

John 16:13,14

To one there is given through the Spirit the message of wisdom, to another the message of knowledge by means of the same Spirit.

1 Corinthians 12:8

I have not stopped giving thanks for you, remembering you in my prayers.

I keep asking that the God of our Lord Jesus Christ, the glorious Father, may give you the Spirit of wisdom and revelation, so that you may know him better.

I pray also that the eyes of your heart may be enlightened in order that you may know the hope to which he has called you, the riches of his glorious inheritance in the saints.

Ephesians 1:16-18

For this reason, since the day we heard about you, we have not stopped praying for you and asking God to fill you with the knowledge of his will through all spiritual wisdom and understanding.

And we pray this in order that you may live a life worthy of the Lord and may please him in every way: bearing fruit in every good work, growing in the knowledge of God.

Colossians 1:9,10

For God did not give us a spirit of timidity, but a spirit of power, of love and of self-discipline.

2 Timothy 1:7

If any of you lacks wisdom, he should ask God, who gives generously to all without finding fault, and it will be given to him.

James 1:5

When You Fail To Meet Your Personal Expectations

"Come," he said. Then Peter got down out of the boat, walked on the water and came toward Jesus.

But when he saw the wind, he was afraid and, beginning to sink, cried out, "Lord, save me!"

Immediately Jesus reached out his hand and caught him. "You of little faith," he said, "why did you doubt?"

Matthew 14:29-31

"If you can?" said Jesus. "Everything is possible for him who believes."

Mark 9:23

He sent them to the Lord to ask, "Are you the one who was to come, or should we expect someone else?"

When the men came to Jesus, they said, "John the Baptist sent us to you to ask, 'Are you the one who was to come, or should we expect someone else?' "

At that very time Jesus cured many who had diseases, sicknesses and evil spirits, and gave sight to many who were blind.

So he replied to the messengers, "Go back and report to John what you have seen and heard: The blind receive sight, the lame walk, those who have leprosy are cured, the deaf hear, the dead are raised, and the good news is preached to the poor.

Blessed is the man who does not fall away on account of me."

Luke 7:19-23

Therefore, my dear brothers, stand firm. Let nothing move you. Always give yourselves fully to the work of the Lord, because you know that your labor in the Lord is not in vain.

1 Corinthians 15:58

Let us not become weary in doing good, for at the proper time we will reap a harvest if we do not give up.

Galatians 6:9

You need to persevere so that when you have done the will of God, you will receive what he has promised.

But my righteous one will live by faith. And if he shrinks back, I will not be pleased with him.

Hebrews 10:36,38

The Lord is not slow in keeping his promise, as some understand slowness. He is patient with you, not wanting anyone to perish, but everyone to come to repentance.

2 Peter 3:9

When You Feel Incapable of Achieving Your Goals and Dreams

I will instruct you and teach you in the way you should go; I will counsel you and watch over you.

Psalm 32:8

For with you is the fountain of life; in your light we see light.

Psalm 36:9

The LORD will fulfill for me; your love, O LORD, endures forever — do not abandon the works of your hands.

Psalm 138:8

Let the wise listen and add to their learning, and let the discerning get guidance.

Proverbs 1:5

Wisdom is supreme; therefore get wisdom. Though it cost all you have, get understanding.

Proverbs 4:7

Esteem her, and she will exalt you; embrace her, and she will honor you.

Proverbs 4:8

Bestowing wealth on those who love me and making their treasuries full.

Proverbs 8:21

The plans of the righteous are just, but the advice of the wicked is deceitful.

Proverbs 12:5

Know also that wisdom is sweet to your soul; if you find it, there is a future hope for you, and your hope will not be cut off.

Proverbs 24:14

See, the former things have taken place, and new things I declare; before they spring into being I announce them to you.

Isaiah 42:9

Forget the former things; do not dwell on the past.

See, I am doing a new thing! Now it springs up; do you not perceive it? I am making a way in the desert and streams in the wasteland.

Isaiah 43:18,19

"For I know the plans I have for you," declares the LORD, "plans to prosper you and not to harm you, plans to give you hope and a future."

Jeremiah 29:11

Then the LORD replied: ''Write down the revelation and make it plain on tablets so that a herald may run with it.

For the revelation awaits an appointed time; it speaks of the end and will not prove false. Though it linger, wait for it; it will certainly come and will not delay.''

Habakkuk 2:2,3

The Sovereign LORD is my strength; he makes my feet like the feet of a deer, he enables me to go on the heights. For the director of music. On my stringed instruments.

Habakkuk 3:19

Ask and it will be given to you; seek and you will find; knock and the door will be opened to you.

Matthew 7:7

Do not be anxious about anything, but in everything, by prayer and petition, with thanksgiving, present your requests to God.

Philippians 4:6

When You Feel Lonely and Unappreciated

Even though I walk through the valley of the shadow of death, I will fear no evil, for you are with me; your rod and your staff, they comfort me.

Psalm 23:4

The LORD is close to the brokenhearted and saves those who are crushed in spirit.

Psalm 34:18

I was young and now I am old, yet I have never seen the righteous forsaken or their children begging bread.

For the LORD loves the just and will not forsake his faithful ones. They will be protected forever, but the offspring of the wicked will be cut off.

Psalm 37:25,28

God is our refuge and strength, an ever-present help in trouble.

Psalm 46:1

He heals the brokenhearted and binds up their wounds.

Psalm 147:3

So do not fear, for I am with you; do not be dismayed, for I am your God. I will strengthen you and help you; I will uphold you with my righteous right hand.

Isaiah 41:10

"Though the mountains be shaken and the hills be removed, yet my unfailing love for you will not be shaken nor my covenant of peace be removed," says the LORD, who has compassion on you.

Isaiah 54:10

And even the very hairs of your head are all numbered.

Matthew 10:30

And teaching them to obey everything I have commanded you. And surely I am with you always, to the very end of the age.

Matthew 28:20

Do not let your hearts be troubled. Trust in God; trust also in me.

And I will ask the Father, and he will give you another Counselor to be with you forever — the Spirit of truth. The world cannot accept

him, because it neither sees him nor knows
him. But you know him, for he lives with you
and will be in you.

I will not leave you as orphans; I will come
to you.

John 14:1,16-18

The Lord will rescue me from every evil
attack and will bring me safely to his heavenly
kingdom. To him be glory for ever and ever.
Amen.

2 Timothy 4:18

For we do not have a high priest who is
unable to sympathize with our weaknesses, but
we have one who has been tempted in every
way, just as we are — yet was without sin.

Let us then approach the throne of grace
with confidence, so that we may receive mercy
and find grace to help us in our time of need.

Hebrews 4:15,16

And be content with what you have,
because God has said, ''Never will I leave you;
never will I forsake you.''

Hebrews 13:5b

Cast all your anxiety on him because he cares for you.

1 Peter 5:7

When You Need to Overcome Anger

Do not be quickly provoked in your spirit, for anger resides in the lap of fools.

Ecclesiastes 7:9

The Sovereign LORD has given me an instructed tongue, to know the word that sustains the weary. He wakens me morning by morning, wakens my ear to listen like one being taught.

Isaiah 50:4

Blessed are the peacemakers, for they will be called sons of God.

Matthew 5:9

The mind of sinful man is death, but the mind controlled by the Spirit is life and peace.

Romans 8:6

The acts of the sinful nature are obvious: sexual immorality, impurity and debauchery; idolatry and witchcraft; hatred, discord, jealousy, fits of rage, selfish ambition, dissensions, factions and envy; drunkenness, orgies, and the like. I warn you, as I did before, that those who live like this will not inherit the kingdom of God.

But the fruit of the Spirit is love, joy, peace, patience, kindness, goodness, faithfulness, gentleness and self-control. Against such things there is no law.

Those who belong to Christ Jesus have crucified the sinful nature with its passions and desires.

Since we live by the Spirit, let us keep in step with the Spirit.

Let us not become conceited, provoking and envying each other.

Galatians 5:19-26

"In your anger do not sin": Do not let the sun go down while you are still angry.

Get rid of all bitterness, rage and anger, brawling and slander, along with every form of malice.

Be kind and compassionate to one another, forgiving each other, just as in Christ God forgave you.

Ephesians 4:26,31,32

Do nothing out of selfish ambition or vain conceit, but in humility consider others better than yourselves.

Each of you should look not only to your own interests, but also to the interests of others.

Philippians 2:3,4

My dear brothers, take note of this: Everyone should be quick to listen, slow to speak and slow to become angry, for man's anger does not bring about the righteous life that God desires.

James 1:19,20

When You Need To Overcome Resentment

Love is patient, love is kind. It does not envy, it does not boast, it is not proud.

It is not rude, it is not self-seeking, it is not easily angered, it keeps no record of wrongs.

1 Corinthians 13:4,5

The weapons we fight with are not the weapons of the world. On the contrary, they have divine power to demolish strongholds.

2 Corinthians 10:4

Get rid of all bitterness, rage and anger, brawling and slander, along with every form of malice.

Ephesians 4:31

Finally, be strong in the Lord and in his mighty power.

Ephesians 6:10

Finally, brothers, whatever is true, whatever is noble, whatever is right, whatever is pure, whatever is lovely, whatever is admirable — if anything is excellent or praiseworthy — think about such things.

Philippians 4:8

Who is wise and understanding among you? Let him show it by his good life, by deeds done in the humility that comes from wisdom.

For where you have envy and selfish ambition, there you find disorder and every evil practice.

James 3:13,16

When You Need To Overcome Envy or Jealousy

Keep your tongue from evil and your lips from speaking lies.

Psalm 34:13

Do not fret because of evil men or be envious of those who do wrong.

Psalm 37:1

Do not envy a violent man or choose any of his ways.

Proverbs 3:31

A heart at peace gives life to the body, but envy rots the bones.

Proverbs 14:30

The tongue has the power of life and death, and those who love it will eat its fruit.

Proverbs 18:21

Do not envy wicked men, do not desire their company.

Proverbs 24:1

Place me like a seal over your heart, like a seal on your arm; for love is as strong as death, its jealousy unyielding as the grave. It burns like blazing fire, like a mighty flame.

Song of Solomon 8:6

Be perfect, therefore, as your heavenly Father is perfect.

Matthew 5:48

Do not judge, or you too will be judged.

Matthew 7:1

Let us behave decently, as in the daytime, not in orgies and drunkenness, not in sexual immorality and debauchery, not in dissension and jealousy.

Romans 13:13

You are still worldly. For since there is jealousy and quarreling among you, are you not worldly? Are you not acting like mere men?

1 Corinthians 3:3

Love is patient, love is kind. It does not envy, it does not boast, it is not proud.

1 Corinthians 13:4

Those who belong to Christ Jesus have crucified the sinful nature with its passions and desires.

Since we live by the Spirit, let us keep in step with the Spirit.

Let us not become conceited, provoking and envying each other.

Galatians 5:24-26

Do not let any unwholesome talk come out of your mouths, but only what is helpful for building others up according to their needs, that it may benefit those who listen.

Get rid of all bitterness, rage and anger, brawling and slander, along with every form of malice.

Ephesians 4:29,31

Therefore, rid yourselves of all malice and all deceit, hypocrisy, envy, and slander of every kind.

Like newborn babies, crave pure spiritual milk, so that by it you may grow up in your salvation.

1 Peter 2:1,2

Do not repay evil with evil or insult with insult, but with blessing, because to this you were called so that you may inherit a blessing.

For, ''Whoever would love life and see good days must keep his tongue from evil and his lips from deceitful speech.''

1 Peter 3:9,10

But you, dear friends, build yourselves up in your most holy faith and pray in the Holy Spirit.

Jude 1:20

When You Feel Anxious About Your Advancing Age

Moses was a hundred and twenty years old when he died, yet his eyes were not weak nor his strength gone.

Deuteronomy 34:7

Surely goodness and love will follow me all the days of my life, and I will dwell in the house of the LORD forever.

Psalm 23:6

They will still bear fruit in old age, they will stay fresh and green.

Psalm 92:14

For they will prolong your life many years and bring you prosperity.

Proverbs 3:2

He gives strength to the weary and increases the power of the weak.

Even youths grow tired and weary, and young men stumble and fall; but those who hope in the LORD will renew their strength. They will soar on wings like eagles; they will run and not grow weary, they will walk and not be faint.

Isaiah 40:29-31

Keep your lives free from the love of money and be content with what you have, because God has said, "Never will I leave you; never will I forsake you."

Hebrews 13:5

When You Feel Used

Those who know your name will trust in you, for you, LORD, have never forsaken those who seek you.

Psalm 9:10

A righteous man may have many troubles, but the LORD delivers him from them all.

Psalm 34:19

"Because he loves me," says the LORD, "I will rescue him; I will protect him, for he acknowledges my name.

He will call upon me, and I will answer him; I will be with him in trouble, I will deliver him and honor him.

Psalm 91:14,15

Trust in the LORD with all your heart and lean not on your own understanding; in all your ways acknowledge him, and he will make your paths straight.

Proverbs 3:5,6

So do not fear, for I am with you; do not be dismayed, for I am your God. I will strengthen you and help you; I will uphold you with my righteous right hand.

Isaiah 41:10

Can a mother forget the baby at her breast and have no compassion on the child she has borne? Though she may forget, I will not forget you!

See, I have engraved you on the palms of my hands; your walls are ever before me.

Isaiah 49:15,16

And surely I am with you always, to the very end of the age.

Matthew 28:20b

I have given you authority to trample on snakes and scorpions and to overcome all the power of the enemy; nothing will harm you.

Luke 10:19

What, then, shall we say in response to this? If God is for us, who can be against us?

Romans 8:31

So we say with confidence, "The Lord is my helper; I will not be afraid. What can man do to me?"

Hebrews 13:6

Cast all your anxiety on him because he cares for you.

1 Peter 5:7

They overcame him by the blood of the Lamb and by the word of their testimony; they did not love their lives so much as to shrink from death.

Revelation 12:11

When You Feel Depressed

For his anger lasts only a moment, but his favor lasts a lifetime; weeping may remain for a night, but rejoicing comes in the morning.

Psalm 30:5

The righteous cry out, and the LORD hears them; he delivers them from all their troubles.

Psalm 34:17

I will praise you, O LORD, with all my heart; before the "gods" I will sing your praise.

Psalm 138:1

Blessed is the man who finds wisdom, the man who gains understanding.

Her ways are pleasant ways, and all her paths are peace.

She is a tree of life to those who embrace her; those who lay hold of her will be blessed.
Proverbs 3:13,17,18

The desert and the parched land will be glad; the wilderness will rejoice and blossom. Like the crocus it will burst into bloom; it will rejoice greatly and shout for joy.
Isaiah 35:1,2

But those who hope in the LORD will renew their strength. They will soar on wings like eagles; they will run and not grow weary, they will walk and not be faint.
Isaiah 40:31

So do not fear, for I am with you; do not be dismayed, for I am your God. I will strengthen you and help you; I will uphold you with my righteous right hand.

Isaiah 41:10

When you pass through the waters, I will be with you; and when you pass through the rivers, they will not sweep over you. When you walk through the fire, you will not be burned; the flames will not set you ablaze.

Isaiah 43:2

Because the Sovereign LORD helps me, I will not be disgraced. Therefore have I set my face like flint, and I know I will not be put to shame.

Isaiah 50:7

For I am convinced that neither death nor life, neither angels nor demons, neither the present nor the future, nor any powers, neither height nor depth, nor anything else in all creation, will be able to separate us from the love of God that is in Christ Jesus our Lord.

Romans 8:38,39

Praise be to the God and Father of our Lord Jesus Christ, the Father of compassion and the God of all comfort, who comforts us in all our troubles, so that we can comfort those in any trouble with the comfort we ourselves have received from God.

2 Corinthians 1:3,4

Dear friends, do not be surprised at the painful trial you are suffering, as though something strange were happening to you.

But rejoice that you participate in the sufferings of Christ, so that you may be overjoyed when his glory is revealed.

1 Peter 4:12,13

When You Feel Sexual Temptation

But you are a shield around me, O LORD; you bestow glory on me and lift up my head.

Psalm 3:3

May integrity and uprightness protect me, because my hope is in you.

Psalm 25:21

Vindicate me, O LORD, for I have led a blameless life; I have trusted in the LORD without wavering.

But I lead a blameless life; redeem me and be merciful to me.

Psalm 26:1,11

Be pleased, O LORD, to save me; O LORD, come quickly to help me.
May all who seek to take my life be put to shame and confusion; may all who desire my ruin be turned back in disgrace.

Psalm 40:13,14

It is better to take refuge in the LORD than to trust in man.

Psalm 118:8

I have hidden your word in my heart that I might not sin against you.

Psalm 119:11

For the LORD will be your confidence and will keep your foot from being snared.
Proverbs 3:26

And lead us not into temptation, but deliver us from the evil one.

Matthew 6:13

Watch and pray so that you will not fall into temptation. The spirit is willing, but the body is weak.

Matthew 26:41

For sin shall not be your master, because you are not under law, but under grace.

Romans 6:14

No temptation has seized you except what is common to man. And God is faithful; he will not let you be tempted beyond what you can bear. But when you are tempted, he will also provide a way out so that you can stand up under it.

1 Corinthians 10:13

Even though my illness was a trial to you, you did not treat me with contempt or scorn. Instead, you welcomed me as if I were an angel of God, as if I were Christ Jesus himself.

Galatians 4:14

You were taught, with regard to your former way of life, to put off your old self, which is being corrupted by its deceitful desires.

Ephesians 4:22

Because he himself suffered when he was tempted, he is able to help those who are being tempted.

Hebrews 2:18

When tempted, no one should say, "God is tempting me." For God cannot be tempted by evil, nor does he tempt anyone; but each one is tempted when, by his own evil desire, he is dragged away and enticed.

James 1:13,14

Be self-controlled and alert. Your enemy the devil prowls around like a roaring lion looking for someone to devour.

Resist him, standing firm in the faith, because you know that your brothers throughout the world are undergoing the same kind of sufferings.

1 Peter 5:8,9

If this is so, then the Lord knows how to rescue godly men from trials and to hold the unrighteous for the day of judgment, while continuing their punishment.

2 Peter 2:9

Since you have kept my command to endure patiently, I will also keep you from the hour of trial that is going to come upon the whole world to test those who live on the earth.

Revelation 3:10

Additional copies of *The Father's Topical Bible* are available from your local bookstore or by writing:

Honor Books • P. O. Box 55388 • Tulsa, OK 74155

INSPIRATIONAL LEATHER GIFT SERIES

The Mother's Topical Bible

The Father's Topical Bible

The Teen's Topical Bible

The Businessman's
Topical Bible

Our Life Together

Dare To Succeed

Image of Excellence

Student's Gold

*Available from your
local bookstore*